The Rules of Disorder

Social Worlds of Childhood

General Editor: Rom Harré

The Rules of Disorder

Peter Marsh
Elisabeth Rosser
Rom Harré

Routledge & Kegan Paul
London, Henley and Boston

First published in 1978
by Routledge & Kegan Paul Ltd
39 Store Street,
London WC1E 7DD,
Broadway House,
Newtown Road,
Henley-on-Thames,
Oxon RG9 1EN and
9 Park Street,
Boston, Mass. 02108, USA
Phototypeset in 10 on 11 pt VIP Times by
Western Printing Services, Ltd, Bristol
and printed in Great Britain by
Lowe & Brydone Printers Ltd
Thetford, Norfolk

British Library Cataloguing in Publication Data

Marsh, Peter
The rules of disorder. – (Social worlds of childhood).
1. Juvenile delinquency   2. Deviant behaviour
I. Title   II. Rosser, Elizabeth   III. Harré, Romano
IV. Series
301.6'2   HQ784.D/   77–30445

ISBN 0 7100 8747 0

General Editor's Preface

For most of us childhood is a forgotten and even a rejected time. The aim of this series is to recover the flavour of childhood and adolescence in a systematic and sympathetic way. The frame of mind cultivated by the authors as investigators is that of anthropologists who glimpse a strange tribe across a space of forest and millennia of time. The huddled group on the other side of the school playground and the thumping of feet in the upstairs rooms mark the presence of a strange tribe. This frame of mind is deliberately different from that of the classical investigators of child psychology, who have brought adult concepts to bear upon the understanding of children's thoughts and actions, and have looked at childhood primarily as a passage towards the skills and accomplishments and distortions of adults. In these studies the authors try to look upon the activities of children as autonomous and complete in themselves. Of course, not all the activities of childhood could be treated in this way. Rather than being in opposition to the traditional kind of study, the work upon which this series is based aims to amplify our understanding by bringing to light aspects of childhood which usually remain invisible when it is looked at in the traditional way. The ethogenic method is in use throughout the studies represented in this series, that is the children themselves are the prime sources of theories about their actions and thoughts and of explanations of the inwardness of their otherwise mysterious activities.

Contents

Acknowledgments

We would like to thank the Directors and staff of Oxford United for their help and full co-operation over the past three years. We also owe a debt to the many school kids and football fans whose social worlds have been the subject of our research. This is their story.

PEM
ER
RH

1
Themes and Anticipations

Introduction

The ostensible subject matter of this book is violence and disorder. Our settings are classrooms and the terraces of football grounds. Our *dramatis personae* are the people who inhabit these places and the people who speak about them in various public ways. Many people believe that there are schoolrooms and football grounds where civilized order is forever on the verge of breaking down. How have they come to believe this? Certainly not by direct experience, for few who 'know' about schoolroom or football violence have been present at its manifestations. Newspaper, radio and television reports are intimately involved in the formation of our images of the places beyond our immediate experience, and the pictures we form of the places featured in our study are no exception. Such reports suggest, often in the choice of vocabulary as much as in overt statement, that classrooms and football grounds are the settings for scenes of anarchy and disorder. But more than that they imply a specific theory about the genesis of social violence. It is the theory that in these special places gaps widen out in the texture of order and without that order uncontrollable impulses lead to meaningless and violent behaviour.

Set against this picture and parallel to the theory that accompanies and supports it is the idea of the possibility of order as a creation of social instruments ordained for that very task, namely teachers, police, social workers, and perhaps, in the last resort, parents.

As we will show, almost nothing of this popular conception survives a thorough examination of the day-to-day practices and the explanations that are vouchsafed for them in vogue among the folk who inhabit these notorious places. Life, as it is lived in classrooms and on the terraces, has almost none of the characteristics of anarchy and impulsiveness that are often attributed to it. As Paul Corrigan shows (Corrigan, forthcoming), even the street corner, as a social place, is not what it seems from a passing vehicle.

Not only do we reveal a different interpretation of what is happening but we propose a very different psychological basis for this activity. We have come to see it through the eyes of the people who take part in it. They see their social life as a struggle for personal dignity in a general social framework that daily denies them this dignity. Far from valuing disorder, they are engaged in the genesis of significance for their lives and an order in their actions that is their own. The struggle begins when they see many of the things that seem routine to the rest of us as ways of devaluing them. The official forms of order can seem anomic to those who are systematically treated as non-persons, since, as they pursue their lives, they have no stake in the society for whose maintenance that order exists. If they are to have any significance, their lives must be self-constructed and *made* significant with the use of homemade materials.

Apprenticeship to Sociality

In what company do people acquire their sense of and competence in the social? The immediate family and the experiences of family living must play a considerable role. But it is certainly not the only locale nor the only company in which competence in and knowledge of the social world is acquired. Talcott Parsons has proposed the very influential theory that of all other available institutions it is the classroom that above all converts an incomplete person into a member of the kind of society Parsons takes for granted as natural, that is, a kind of society where to be social is to be interested in achievement.

At the basis of Parsons's theory is a contrast between family life and school life. School life is lived in a society that is constituted in the course of lessons. The form it takes is very much in accordance with structuring principles imposed by the teacher. In the family, as in the classroom, there is a dominant role player, usually the mother. The central person is revealed by identifying the sources of rewards and privileges. At home rewards are 'ascriptive', depending on who one is rather than on what one does. What is given as a satisfying offering from the dominant person is roughly related to needs. In the classroom, on the other hand, getting and giving is more nearly related to achievement. Effort is the source of good things, if only one can get one's efforts recognized by the dominant person in the situation. In these ways, despite differences, schoolroom and home are continuously related to one another as social places. But since there are much larger numbers in relation to the dominant person in the schoolroom than there are at home a distinct psychological break is experienced in the transition from one to the other. Parsons believes that in the schoolroom the children acquire their attachment to the larger social order of adult society which is reflected in the methods of giving and getting encouraged in school. As schooling goes on there is a progressive revelation of the selective role of the school *vis-à-vis* the labour market, bringing children into an asymptotic relation to 'real life', for which it provides the apprenticeship. According to Parsons, criminality arises in the feral life of the playground.

We would turn this picture upside down. The social structure of the society of the classroom seems to us as well adapted to be the nursery of crime as it is of 'good' behaviour. The distinction between real and apparent achievement, if only it can be concealed from the teacher, and suitably managed by a child, provides the opportunity for rewards to be received just as well for cheating as for genuine achievement. The possibility of achieving the semblance of virtue by working at standing high in the teacher's estimation, seems to us a perfect nursery for the acquisition of the criminal or exploitative view of the social world.

Parsons has socialized the official theory of the school and schooling without enquiry into its legitimacy or exclusiveness as a social theory of school.

But if the commonsense understanding of schooling is bracketed and belief suspended, another reality emerges, the life of the playground. There, we believe, are constructed fragments of society the reality of which is unquestioned by the children who are its constructors and who know how to maintain it. It is a world of compacts and bargains, of the control of present and future by ritual, a world dominated by the absolute power of words once spoken to bring order to the world of actions and social relations, an order which needs other words to dispel. Here, if anywhere, lies true sociality, and the place of apprenticeship, for here oaths are really binding and rules need no sanction for their consent. Here there can be no crime for it is a world built by all for all. Deviation is managed and progressively denied by continual renegotiation of the social reality against which it is set off. In the chapters to come, contrast if you will the demanding world of the schoolroom, as our participants see it, with the world of ritual and formal genesis of a respected self in the putting on of the regalia of the club that reigns on the terraces.

Attributions: The Multiplicity of Rhetorics

A complex society usually includes a number of microsocieties whose ways of assigning meaning to their actions are not universally nor even very widely shared in the community. In such a situation the possibility exists for attributions of meaning to be made to the deeds of members of the microsociety which bear little resemblance to the meanings attributed by the members themselves. An intuition that this is indeed so may be very difficult to substantiate if the attributions made by members of the dominant society are very loud and very visible, and those of the members of the microsociety hard to come by, perhaps because those members are not easy to contact. There are many examples of this situation in contemporary Britain, such as the case of some schoolchildren, many gypsies and almost all football fans. We shall distinguish attributions as external when made by members of the dominant society to the deeds of members of the microsociety, and as internal when attributions are made by members to deeds of their own or of other members of the microsociety to which they belong.

External attributions may take two forms:
1   That there is no meaning to be attached to the members' actions. An article in the *Oxford Times* of 18 May 1976 describes an encounter between a householder and a group of rather tiresome young people who had chosen his street frontage as a meeting place. Trouble grew between the family whose house was beleaguered each night and the unwelcome street visitors. We shall be drawing upon this case further, but for the moment we want to draw attention only to the way in which the reporter, by a particular choice of descriptive vocabulary, conveyed the impression that the actions of the group were meaningless. They were described as 'shouting and screaming'. While one may reasonably ask what someone shouted, it hardly makes sense to ask what it was they screamed. So the conjunction of these two words effectively prevents the raising of the question as to what it was that they were saying. Their vocalizations are consigned to the category of mere noise.
2   That the activities of some young people, particularly adolescents, are not to be explained in terms of the ordinary, rational rule-following upon which we pride ourselves, but as springing from primitive, almost animal-like impulses and drives. In this mode of attribution young people are not spoken of as having tragic love affairs, rather it is said that 'they can't cope with physical sexual experiences'. On the following page is a newspaper report as an illustration of this mode of attribution.

Girl who dies 'could not cope with sex'
A girl pupil at Millfield School began having sex at 14, an inquest was told yesterday. But early maturity led to her killing herself.

Mr. Daniel Williams, the coroner at the inquest at Honiton, said Joanna Burrell, aged 15, could not cope with her physical sexual experiences 'divorced from any continuing permanent affection'.

She had lain on her bed at her farmhouse home on January 2 and put a double-barrelled shotgun to her head.

Recording a verdict that she killed herself, Mr. Williams said: 'She was an affectionate girl, and a girl who needed affection. She was a young and sensitive girl growing up, and she found things too much for her.'

The sentence 'Early maturity led to her killing herself' suggests an organic disorder, rather than a human tragedy. Had we had her account available our guess is that it would have been expressed in such a way as to suggest a quite different kind of story, where personal rather than biological matters were at issue.

The same sort of attribution, of urges out of control, is a recurring theme in the reporting of school violence. Here we can turn to a report by Tim Devlin in *The Times* of 6 May 1975. A teacher is reported as speaking in the following way: 'Two huge girls were fighting. I was really frightened they would hurt each other. I could not stop them, so I rather let them get on with it. . . .' This could be read equally as 'Two huge bears were . . .' and the picture would not be essentially different. No sense of a sharing in the social meaning of what was going on emerges, and we daresay the unfortunate teacher, with whose plight we do indeed sympathize, did not have the faintest idea what was afoot. But what was afoot was not an encounter between natural forces, or even animals, but *people*.

The same rhetoric appears with great frequency in the description of the football scene. Here are some examples:

Soccer Hooligans Run Riot
Violence erupted at the . . . Public House . . . the landlord said 'It was terrifying'.

Fence Them In
British soccer's first spiked steel fence will form an impenetrable barrier to unruly . . . fans next season.

Where Were the Tartan Terrors?
The loudly heralded Tartan Terror on the road to Wembley failed to show up yesterday. Londoners discovered that despite the dire

predictions, the Scots might look a bit terrifying, but they were more interested in the goings-on at Wembley.

Smash These Thugs
Rees pledge after soccer terror trip.

Clobber Boys on the Rampage

However, some reporting is more sophisticated. Under the heading 'Wild Ones of the Terraces', a typical piece of the standard rhetoric, a fan was allowed to speak for himself. 'We fight for the pride of our ends' he explained. 'What's so marvellous, is that these kids who are doing bum jobs, and are said to be idiots, can get themselves organized like this, and set up a fabulous military strategy that goes into battle.'

We shall show that, contrary to popular opinion, the 'kids' are knowledgeable about their situation and the meaning of their actions, and are capable of deploying a high standard of theorizing about their activities. They show considerable linguistic and conceptual sophistication. In short, they have an explanatory rhetoric at their command. But it is different from that of the media. The latter both reflects and influences the speech forms and the conceptual resources of those who describe what are essentially alien lives from the outside. The existence of two rhetorics, of two different systems of understanding and explanation at such odds with one another, leads to a situation in which the lives and aspirations, wishes and needs of each company become more and more opaque to each other.

A contrary point of view has been maintained in a very popular socio-linguistic theory which has had considerable recent currency. This is Bernstein's theory of restricted and elaborated codes (Bernstein, 1971). Roughly, the theory claims that 'working-class' children, those with whom we have been speaking in preparing this study, are suffering from a linguistic and cognitive defect *vis-à-vis* their 'middle-class' counterparts. According to Bernstein, the very conditions of their upbringing lead to their being linguistically crippled. Their language is a restricted code, so they will not be able to formulate and hence will not be able to understand many of the things which middle-class children can formulate and understand. Mental horizons will be restricted because linguistic resources are restricted.

The distinction between a restricted and an elaborated code is based on language studies carried out by middle-class investigators who entered the social world of 'working-class' children from the outside and *without credentials* valid in that world. Not surprisingly, communication was simplified and rudimentary forms dominated the interactions, as those imposed upon adopted the time-old tactic of retreating into inarticulateness to conceal what goes on within their life-world. This social tactic leads to the idea that linguistic deficit has been established empirically. The theory was rounded off by the idea that the structure and content of the curriculum as practised in any school whatever, formal or free-form was to the advantage of those capable of indefinite linguistic and conceptual elaboration. It will become clear in the course of our exposition that our studies do not support this theory. There is no evidence of linguistic deficit. Everything depends upon the situation in which talk and theorizing takes place, and between whom it is created, and what it is about. There are, however, great differences in linguistic style between academically and non-academically oriented children.

We are forced to conclude that each microsociety has its own elaborated code, capable of indefinite extension, but that it presents an opaque front to the confrontation surfaces of other microsocieties. Opacity is a social creation, a device of resistance, achieved by the closing down of speech till it has all the appearances of a restricted code. In the rudimentary forms of communication which are the only survivors of the closing-down process, very few issues indeed can be addressed.

A striking example of the growth of opacity is to be found in the story we have already referred to, as reported in the *Oxford Mail*. The episode as reported, involved a confrontation between a family, let us call them the Joneses, and a number of young people. These young people, much like a flock of birds, settled along the Joneses' street frontage. The newspaper reports the affair wholly within the rhetoric of the Joneses. We have no record in the newspaper of an account from the point of view of the 'kids'. Their rhetoric is not represented.

Our interpretation of the predicament of the Joneses is simple. Each side generates a discourse that is powerless and almost meaningless in the linguistic world of the other. Mr Jones's attempts to control the situation by speech, his speech forms being in all probability in the mode of command, are reported as leading amazingly rapidly to the offer of violence. Can this have been the opening phases of the interaction? Hardly. Mr Jones's reported 'telling-them-to-go' belongs in a mode of speech instantly recognizable by the folk of the flock as part of the rhetoric of the very world they are closed to. No doubt there was speech addressed from them to him – speech he now glosses as 'greeting with abuse and swearing'. How could this situation fail to develop if he 'failed to stop the nuisance by appealing to the parents of the young people'? It is just their dignity as selves that is at issue, and Mr Jones has chosen the most powerful humiliation of all, that is treating them as within the social control of their parents.

At this stage nothing remains but that each should present an opaque front to the other. Mr Jones issues orders – the kids offer simplified abuse. Each has *achieved* opacity by progressive restriction of their modes of communication. The kids see Mr Jones as incapable of anything but command, Mr Jones sees the kids as incapable of anything but abuse. The newspaper reporter fails both sides to the dispute by adopting the rhetoric of only one of them, that of Mr Jones. But then Mr Jones has access to the reporter and to the apparatus of public statement in a way that the kids manifestly do not.

We are not suggesting that it was a good thing that a flock of kids roosted on Mr Jones's garden fence. They must have been a bloody nuisance. But the situation was not as the newspaper led its readers to believe, that is the articulate Mr Jones and the feral flock of savages locked in primitive combat. Two cultures confronted one another, each, as we shall show, capable of elaboration within.

Sometimes a theory is forcibly 'shared', either by reason of the rhetorical power of its promoters, or more rarely by exacting physical penalties from those who demur. Outside the imaginations of well-meaning social scientists and novelists that sort of situation is rare. Mostly master and slave *share* a theory. And the reverberations of that shared theory may last for a very long time, long after the institution which was its natural concomitant in day-to-day social practices has gone. A striking example of this is the passive 'loser' social style of many American black people, the style that black militants have tried with some desperation and success to redress. It reflects a conception of themselves inherited from the theory of their nature and place in a slave society, a theory they shared with the slave owners, and from whom they learned it. Depersonalization rituals, including the conditions on the voyage from Africa and the ritual humiliations of their inauguration to the plantation society have been carefully detailed in modern historical studies of the institution. In our case too, pupils and teachers share the theory that the pupils are 'written off'. We do not know how this shared theory came to be acquired. Labelling theory has revealed something of the genesis of individual theories of the self in society, but we know little about the mechanisms and occasions of large-scale learning of such things.

Moral Panic

Neither the use of different rhetorical systems nor the genesis of mutual opacity to understand can explain the force and indeed the extravagant character of the attributions imposed upon disenchanted and rebellious schoolchildren and rumbustious football fans. To explain this we introduce Stan Cohen's concept of 'moral panic'.

Societies appear subject, every now and then, to periods of moral panic. A condition, episode, person or group of persons emerges to become defined as a threat to societal values and interests; its nature is presented in a stylised and stereotypical fashion by the media; the moral barricades are manned by editors, bishops, politicians and other right-thinking people; socially accredited experts pronounce their diagnoses and solutions; ways of coping are evolved or (more often) resorted to; the condition then disappears, submerges or deteriorates and becomes more visible. Sometimes the object of the panic is quite novel and at other times it is something which has been in existence long enough, but suddenly appears in the limelight. Sometimes the panic passes over and is forgotten, except in folklore and collective memory; at other times it has more serious and long-lasting repercussions and might produce such changes as those in legal and social policy or even in the way that society conceives itself (S. Cohen, 1972).

Since the war, a succession of moral panics have spread through our society, each with its characteristic 'object'. These objects have ranged historically from Teddy Boys through to Mods and Rockers and Skinheads. The most recent are the football hooligans, who for many people, and not least the feature writers of our Sunday newspapers, have come to represent all that is most senseless and destructive in our society.* Anyone doubting such a claim should simply scan, as we have done, headlines of the more popular newspapers from about 1968 onwards and note the frequency with which terms such as 'mindless', 'evil', 'thuggery', 'mad', 'violent', 'wanton destruction', etc., crop up in reports concerning football supporters. From reading such reports one might be forgiven for thinking that the football terraces ran deep with blood each Saturday and that fans of Manchester United, like Protestants in parts of rural Spain, really do have horns on their heads.

From a transactional sociological viewpoint, the function of Folk Devils is quite clear. In setting up certain members as visible examples of what is proscribed, by attributing forbidden characteristics to them, they serve as images of disorder and evil. Having created

---

* Since the completion of this text, Punks have joined hooligans as a foc'ıs of moral panic (see Marsh, 1977).

these images, our society is more able to ascribe to the majority of its members – the right-thinking corpus – a comforting sense of order and social propriety.

This is not a new message, but in trying to develop a more sensitive account of what contemporary Folk Devils are actually *doing*, we are obliged to consider how and why others in society have come to think of them as doing something quite different. Whilst this is not a strong issue when discussing the allegedly anarchic wrecking of school classrooms (since we have yet to reach the stage where we cast the entire school population as outsiders) it is a crucial one in the discussion of the genesis of the football hooligan. It is against a background of near hysteria that we set out to propose an alternative account of what is happening on the football terraces – an account based not on the second-hand rhetoric of myth-creating media men but on our faith in people's ability to render their own social action intelligible and meaningful.

The driving force behind the transactional approach with which we undertake a study of the fans is, of course, Howard Becker, and although this is not the place to enter into a long discussion of his contribution to a more radical sociology, some brief attention must be given to his work (Becker, 1963). We hope it will be sufficient to point out that we draw from Becker, via Pollner and others, the useful contrast between 'inside' and 'outside' models. The outside model of Becker is the one which has become popular under the title of 'labelling theory' and which has seriously challenged the traditional approaches to the study of so-called deviance. According to this model, deviance is a property which is created and sustained by a community's response to an act as deviant. The deviance lies not in the act itself but is a consequence of the application by 'moral entrepreneurs' of rules and sanctions to the offender. The obvious correctness of this argument can easily be demonstrated by near-to-hand examples. Vandalism, for example, might be thought of as a collection of clearly identifiable acts requiring sanction for the simple reason that they offend against the property, both individual and collective, of members in society. But contrast the reaction to football fans who run through a town creating damage as they go with the reaction to university students during rag week creating similar damage. The former damage will be viewed as the result of 'destructive hooliganism' and dealt with accordingly, whilst the latter will be seen as arising from an excess of good-natured high spirits and over-enthusiasm. Although the damaging acts are very similar, football fans are 'deviants' whilst students, for reasons not made explicit, are somehow excused. We might also note that what constitutes an offence in legal terms also changes over time. Acts such as those involving homosexuality or abortion would, only a few years ago, have been held up as examples of 'hardcore' deviance. And yet those same acts today escape formal sanction. Clearly the relativistic approach of Becker is self-evidently required in one form or another in any sociology of deviance, and it is perhaps a rather miserable reflection on the state of the discipline that such an elementary argument is ignored by those who see it as clashing with their struggle for admission to the club of natural science.

On its own, this outside model is insufficient for our purposes. Whilst it rightly steers us away from naive and simplistic causal theories of deviance, it can hardly provide an approach which is substantially more fruitful. But implicit in what Becker has to say is the 'inside' model, and it is in the juxtaposition of inside and outside models that more realistic explanations are to be found.

Becker hints at the inside model when he concludes, not without generating some confusion, that 'whether a given act is deviant or not depends in part on the nature of the act (that is, whether or not it violates some rule) and in part on what other people do about it'. We see here a move away from the view that deviance is simply what people so label, to the notion that it might also have something to do with the acts that 'deviants' engage in. The problem, however, is that Becker fails to reconcile to any acceptable degree what appear to be two mutually antagonistic themes. Pollner, on the other hand, by adding some flesh to the skeletal possibilities implied by Becker, provides us with a working summary of an approach which yields both sociological and social-psychological perspectives:

> Seen from the 'inside' of an already symbolic universe, 'deviance' presents itself as a property inhering in the acts so characterised. Yet when viewed from the 'outside', the 'deviance' that such acts are deemed to possess is assured only by virtue of a community's orientation to them as wrong, immoral, evil, etc. From within, deviance is an objective property of the act, whereas from without deviance is brought into the world by the communal response (Pollner, 1974).

Following this, it is clear that an understanding of any 'deviant' phenomena will require two avenues of investigation. The first involves a sociological theory of societal creation of deviance and the processes by which this is achieved. The second requires a social psychology of the symbolic universe in which acts are endowed with meaning and the commonsense accounts which are offered within such a universe to render the imposed concept of deviance intelligible. The task for us is the second of these – the presentation of the 'inside' social world of the football fan and uncontrollable schoolchild. But our task is made relevant only in the context of an adequate sociological model which provides for an account, from 'without', of the processes by which football fans come to be viewed as deviant, and how fans come to be portrayed as disordered and devilish. Such a model, we suggest, might well be found in deviancy amplification theory.

Deviancy amplification is achieved by means of a relatively simple positive feedback loop. In its basic form, as proposed by Leslie Wilkins (1964), societal reactions to initial, and often minor, acts of alleged deviance, have the effect of producing some degree of isolation and alienation among those who commit such acts. This in turn leads to a reaction on the part of the deviants which usually involves an increase in the frequency or intensity of the deviant acts. Societal reactions increase as a result and from then on the system feeds on itself. A specialized version of this is the cycles of retribution we have identified in school.

Such a model, in this bare form, is too mechanistic to be of real value. Deviants cannot be viewed as billiard balls inescapably moved by the social forces that surround them. Jock Young (1971), however, following Matza, points out that no such mechanistic assumptions are required for the model. He sees the deviant group as creating its own circumstances to the extent that it makes meaningful the societal reactions to it, or better generates meaning for itself in a world whose societal reactions deny them the full status of persons. Within society the agencies of law and order, and those in a position to sustain the hegemonic ideology, constitute 'controllers'. Both the controllers and the deviant group construct tacit theories in order to explain each other, and such theories are put to the test in interactions between them but never by both groups together. Each tests its own theory. Occasions for such testing occur, for example, during police v. football fan conflicts in and around soccer grounds, in the editorial comments of the media, on the streets and in the classrooms where, whatever teachers may intend, their actions are interpreted as contempt. According to the feedback model, the hypotheses of the controllers about football fans, and of the football fans about the mentality of the controllers, will determine the direction and intensity of the amplification process. Inevitably, however, through selective perceptions of action and reaction, the two sets of hypotheses will often receive verification and confirmation. The resultant hardening of attitudes and images is the stuff from which myths and stereotypes are made.

The main elements of the deviancy amplification process are shown schematically in Figure 1.

Positive feedback systems such as the one outlined, can serve as very useful explanatory devices in social science, and we shall have recourse to another such system later. At the moment we have some idea of the motives for casting certain groups in society as 'outsiders'. We also have some idea of how casting might be achieved. Such ideas we take to form the basis for an adequate sociological

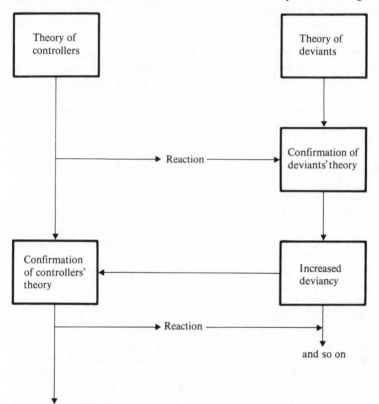

Figure 1
(Source: Jock Young in Stan Cohen (ed.), Images of Deviance, *p. 52).*

model, alongside which we seek to propose our inside account. It should be noted, however, that we will not be concerned with an explanation of why football fans and 'non-academic pupils' as opposed to other groups of boys and girls have come to be cast in this way. It may very well be that the socio-political theory of Ian Taylor, who suggests that soccer hooliganism results from fans being alienated from their football clubs, provides for a correct analysis. As football has become a big-business enterprise in this country, and since the players, who once were seen as members of the same working-class community as the fans themselves, have ecome rich superstars, the close identity between fans and their team has been eroded. Contemporary 'problems' on the terraces can thus be seen, in this historical context, as a coherent resistance of change and as an attempt by fans to reclaim their soccer heritage.

The origins of deviant groups will clearly have a distinct socio-historical context, and analysis of such a context may very well be of considerable explanatory value. But in general, we feel that such explanations need not be particularly powerful. Having accepted that deviance can become amplified through a positive feedback mechanism, and that the initial acts of deviance on which the system feeds are often quite minor, only a relatively weak explanation of the original deviance is called for. We might even go so far as to say that amplification of deviance among one group rather than among another could simply be due to chance. An analogy can be drawn with the notion of mutations in genetics. Here a few chance changes in genetic structure, often quite minor in themselves, can result in a dramatic change in the phylogeny of a given species. Similarly, what we might call a 'social accident', can result in radical alterations of relations within society. Most importantly, even though such 'accidents' may be shown to have had some precipitating social factors in the past, there is no need to suggest that such factors are present today. Once such factors have done their work, the feedback system takes over and itself constitutes an adequate explanation, as an 'outside' model.

In presenting an inside account of social order on the terraces and in the classroom attention is given to an elaboration of the social structures existing among young fans and trouble-makers and the role positions available to members. The data for this elaboration come mainly from a participant observation study at Oxford United and from conversations at a local youth club, but data from other grounds are included to show that Oxford United is far from being an isolated case. Rather, it will be suggested that many of the structures described are more or less 'universal' within the football culture as a whole. Life in other schools is described in another volume of this series. In Paul Corrigan's study *Doing Nothing* he suggests that 'trouble in school' is more or less the same elsewhere.

Actions, Acts and Social Knowledge

The studies to be reported here are based upon a quite specific theory about the relation between social action and individual knowledge of the social world. A person's social life is seen as involving two kinds of performances. There are the actions he or she contributes to the total social process, and there are the accounts in which action is interpreted, criticized and justified. The fundamental ethogenic hypothesis that links acting and accounting is the idea that an individual's ability to do either depends upon his stock of social knowledge. Such knowledge forms a single system in each individual person so that his actions and his accounts are performances drawing only upon one corpus of knowledge. This knowledge is revealed in different ways of acting and in accounting since each is directed to a different end. Actions are the means by which we accomplish social acts, while accounts serve to make what we do intelligible and justified. Our studies are aimed at revealing this knowledge and exploring its structure. The organized system of social knowledge each individual possesses for social performances corresponds to the competence linguists attribute to speakers of a language. The concept of 'competence' as it is used in linguistics corresponds to our idea of individual social knowledge and belief.

Our work is aimed primarily at discovering the content and organization of the social knowledge and belief an individual member has to have, to be able to perform reasonably adequately in the social life of his group. We are not proposing a theory of how a typical member generates his performance on the basis of this knowledge. There will be occasional hints at a theory of performance but they should be taken very hypothetically. To develop a theory of the production of action we would have to introduce the concept of intention explicitly at the level of action. This we do not propose to do. Our participants intend the ends, that is to humiliate a teacher, a social act they accomplish singly or together. We do not know enough to claim that they as consciously intend the means, the specific actions and speeches they produce to accomplish such a social act. In talking of rules we are not offering a psychological theory of performance. At best the idea of action as produced by the following of a rule is an icon or model of the process by which actions are really generated. Of course such a stage is an essential preliminary to the formulation of a theory of the performance of action. Theories in the traditional natural sciences are usually based upon icons of generative processes rather than knowledge of the generative processes themselves, and we are not unhappy to be in that company. Like chemist and physicist we hope one day to be able to find out whether our icons are truly representative of reality. Rules do really appear in accounts concerning the interpretation and justification of action. But in generalizing the concept to the context of the control of action, 'rule-following' must be treated as a metaphor.

Rules of Interpretation and Rules of Action

The concept of rule as an explanatory device has gained wide currency in the social sciences. There remains, however, considerable debate concerning how a rule might be precisely defined and how such a construct can be properly applied to the study of social behaviour. (For a full consideration of this topic see the collection of essays in Collett (1977).) Whilst we recognize the conceptual problems associated with rules and their application, the approach in the ethogenic study of the football and classroom cultures has been a pragmatic one. To assert that conduct is orderly is, from our point of view, to imply that it is directed by a sense of social propriety – that not only is it non-random but that it is both generated and limited by prescriptions and the possibility of sanction, in particular the sanction of expressed disapproval. For example, someone who accepts the official theory of life in the classroom and 'wants to learn' can be heavily sanctioned with abusive appellations from the same stock as are applied to the opposition on the terraces (cf. Chapter 3).

The concept of 'rule' is used here in a 'strong' sense – that is, as something held (although often tacitly) by all members of a group or community as representations of legitimacy and acceptability. Implicit in the holding of such rules are notions of *ought* and *should*. Such rules are not mere statistical abstractions but are directly discoverable, as we will attempt to show, in the accounts which football fans and schoolroom 'trouble makers' offer in explaining what they do and why they do it. Following this, it is clear that a strong distinction can be made between rule on the one hand and normative regularity on the other. Whilst the straightforward observation of overt activity on the football terraces and of cycles of retribution in school will provide evidence of certain invariant sequences and patterns of behaviour, it remains an empirical question as to whether such regularities are the product of rule-following.

In general, two kinds of rule will be considered – first, rules of interpretation and second, prescriptive rules. The distinction is in line with the Kantian contrast between constitutive and regulative rules. Rules of interpretation are thought to be effective in the orderly ascription of meaning to objects and events. They are involved in the way things are defined and made sense of. Prescriptive rules, on the other hand, are seen as directions for action. They are the rules which enable members to choose between possible modes of conduct available to them and to maintain a sense of propriety and social legitimacy. Put simply, rules of interpretation are to be found in answers to questions such as 'What is going on?' or 'What does this mean?', whilst prescriptive rules are to be found through asking 'What should one do?' These two kinds of rule are not, of course, independent of each other. Indeed, before one can decide what action is appropriate one requires an understanding of the social context in which one is acting and an interpretation of the actions occurring in that context. Rules of interpretation, in attaching meaning to situations and their constituents, determine which prescriptive rules are applicable. Action on the basis of such prescription, however, can subsequently lead to changing definitions of the situation which in turn will alter the directions of conduct. Prescriptions presuppose interpretations, but actions on the basis of such prescriptions become themselves the subject of interpretation.

The strongest test for the existence of a rule is the ability of a member of a group to articulate the rule. A person may, in giving an account of his actions, appeal to the existence of a rule in justifying what he did. He might say that there was a convention relating to such actions or that he did something because it was expected of him. He may even suggest, as many football fans do, that there is an 'unwritten law' which either impelled or restricted actions – certain things were either 'done' or 'not done', and everybody in the group knew it.

Where a person offers a rule in this manner, it is reasonable to assume that the rule constitutes a reason for his actions, and in trying to make sense of the world of the football fan it is reasons, rather than causes, which we are seeking. In many instances, however, it would be unreasonable to expect people to be readily able to articulate the rules which guide their behaviour. Many of the routine social situations we find ourselves in are clearly rule-governed, but it is often extremely difficult to specify exactly what the rules are or what are the *potential* breaches of the rules. We can, however, instantly recognize the actual instances where rules are broken. In everyday language we used phrases such as 'he behaved inappropriately' or 'she should know that she can't wear trousers here', or even 'it's not cricket!' When unequivocal recognition of an impropriety can be *interpreted* as the perception of an action as a breaching of a rule, we have a further sufficient condition for asserting that actions are rule-governed.

In addition to the above criteria of articulation and recognition of breaches, a further necessary condition must be satisfied: actions can only be said to be rule-governed when some other alternative actions are possible. In other words, action which is predetermined by some external constraints cannot be seen in the same light as action which accords with some convention, though, on occasion, constrained action may be *glossed* as rule-governed in an associated account, particularly where the agency of a person is in doubt.

Certain actions of football fans, for example, are quite clearly directed by factors extrinsic to their group. One would not want to suggest that attending football games on Saturdays, as opposed to any other day, was rule-governed if matches are only ever played on Saturdays. Rules are arbitrary in character and are to do with the manner in which people choose between *alternative* modes of conduct.

As we are using the notion rules are to be seen as having all-or-none character – if a rule governs a kind of action such action is always governed by rule. We are reluctant to accept that rules can be formulated as probabilistic statements. That a rule can take the form of a statement 'Given P, then Q on 75 per cent of occasions', as is sometimes seriously suggested, is to use the concept of rule in a very dangerous and misleading way. Furthermore, rules are not necessarily predictive of behaviour in any straightforward manner. Their primary role is explanatory. A person's actions can be explained in terms of his following of tacit conventions, but our knowledge of the rules will not allow us to predict what he will do at any given time. Even if one thought that the pursuit of such predictions was useful, a great deal more information would be required, including a knowledge of the extent to which the rules were broken. Indeed, we suspect that a rule which was never broken would not be a rule in our sense at all but rather an inevitability with the logical status of a law.

A consequence of seeing rules in this way is that a very high degree of consensus concerning the rule is to be expected among members of the group or sub-culture in which the rule applies. Social conventions would clearly be of little use if only a small proportion of members was aware of them, and the same holds for the interpretative rules which guide the manner in which meanings are attached to objects and situations. Social order presupposes that members of a group have a common knowledge of rules. The determination of such a consensus, however, is not without its problems. We are faced, in the examination of justificatory accounts, with varying degrees of social knowledge and competence and, as we shall demonstrate, accounts themselves often appear to contain grave inconsistencies and internal contradictions. Happily, such problems are not insoluble and it is towards a stage where we are able to make sense out of sometimes enigmatic statements by fans that a discovery procedure is directed.

Moral Careers

An individual's life in society can be described in a variety of ways, economic, ecological, etc. For our purposes the most apposite is the description of a course of life in terms of the growth of reputation or the loss of public standing undergone by an individual as he or she meets this or that social hazard. A hazard is an occasion on which an individual can gain the respect or risk the contempt of his fellows. Some people seek out occasions of hazard, others shrink from them.

The character or reputation a person has amongst his fellows is partly a product of his own efforts at self-presentation, partly an ascription to him by others on the basis of their readings of his life performances, partly in situations which can be seen as occasions of hazard.

Goffman has described how institutions offer individuals a framework for a moral career. In his well-known work on asylums (Goffman, 1961) he shows how progress through the wards of a mental hospital can be looked upon as a progress through a system of hazards in the course of which honour and reputation is risked, gained and lost. Sometimes a person may have to conceal parts of his past life, or even some of his own present physical charac-teristics, what Goffman (1963) has called stigmata, in order not to jeopardize his reputation in the eyes of others. We follow him in treating these aspects of the life course as a moral career, since they are concerned with a person's reputation, a kind of continuous summing up of his life in terms of what sort of person he is supposed by his fellows to be.

Most institutions offer an offical life trajectory in terms of which honour can be acquired and reputation gained. A school offers a complex, officially recognized and indeed officially defined prog-ress, closely related to the official theory of the school as a place for learning. There may be a second official moral career based upon prowess at officially recognized games. There are honour boards, special clothes, badges, privileges and so on, varying from school to school, in which the results of success at the officially sanctioned occasions of hazard are displayed (Bernstein, 1971). Most institu-tions also have an underlife, defining other forms of moral career with other occasions of hazard and other ways of rendering honour and marking reputation. In the underlife official values are denied. Those who subscribe to them and are honoured by reference to them may be thought of with contempt by those for whom the underlife is the serious basis of social living. This book is mostly concerned with underlives, with those whose moral careers, for one reason or another, are lived in accordance with an unofficial con-ception of social progress.

The Method

The Intensive Design

In the traditional natural sciences generality is achieved in two different ways, each based upon a particular choice of the informal inverse relation between the intension and extension of a class. By supposing that one has a typical member to investigate one can maximize one's knowledge of the properties and structure common to each member of the class by examining that one member in great detail. If, however, one is uncertain about the typical choice of a typical member one may examine all the members one can reach and then form some kind of average, discovering the type that way. The certainty that the average is a type is paid for by the relatively few properties which are likely to survive a generalizing procedure over many individuals. On the other hand, the detail of the knowledge achieved in the use of the intensive design has to be paid for by the ever-present possibility that the case one chose was not typical. Thus the risk is greater when one adopts the intensive design but the pay-off is correspondingly larger.

The extensive method is sure but shallow, the intensive deep but hazardous. Some natural sciences, confident of the uniformity of their objects of study, have adopted the intensive design. In chemistry the initial processes of purification are supposed to ensure that the sample is uncontaminated, and the processes of selection and isolation of materials, that it is typical. Hence, chemical studies are confidently carried out on one or at most a very few instances of the materials that chemists are analysing and synthesizing. The possibility of establishing a taxon or class by fiat encourages anatomists to take one or a few specimens and subject them to very detailed dissection.

In the ethogenic approach we follow the example of chemists and anatomists and adopt the intensive design, that is, we undertake a detailed study of a few cases selected as typical. We are sure of the detailed validity of our analyses of our cases. We can only hypothesize that they are typical. Those who would follow the extensive design can be sure that their results are typical, but they must hypothesize as to whether the few properties that survive the working of the inverse ratio between extension and intension have any individuality at all (De Waele and Harré, 1976).

Our football-following participants are from one group of fans, supporters of just one local club. With few exceptions the participants in our study of talk about classroom violence and its accounting are from one school that is graced by some of the fans.

We are inclined to think they are pretty typical, given our less detailed work at other football grounds and what we know of other groups of schoolchildren.

Interpretation of Actions and the Analysis of Accounts

Our theory is based on the idea that human social life is a product of an interaction between sequences of actions and talk about those actions. Everything we do can be redone by talk. In the course of talk our actions can be redefined and in the process are transformed. Many of the consequences of our acts can be reversed or nullified by redefinition. The rituals of apology can ameliorate the effects of social accidents. Things once done can be undone.

Speech is involved both in the genesis and maintenance of the social world in action-sequences and in the correction and interpretation of that world in accounts, the speech in which we discourse about the action. Acts can be performed by saying something just as well as by doing something. Sometimes a wave can express gratitude as successfully as saying 'Thanks'.

Since the basic hypothesis of the ethogenic approach to the understanding of social action is that the very same social knowledge and skill is involved in the genesis of action and of accounts, by recording and analysing each separately, we have two mutually supporting and reciprocally checking ways of discovering the underlying system of social knowledge and belief.

A further corollary which has figured largely in our studies is the idea that the best, though not necessarily the ultimate, authorities as to what the action 'actually' is, are the actors themselves. In their accounts are to be found, *prima facie*, the best interpretations of what went on, from the standpoint of the problem of the interpretation of action. This follows almost directly from the fact that the actors were the ones who intended the action in the first place. But what about the fact that people lie, that they are perfectly capable of remaking the record to appear in a good light? In particular, what about the point that people like to appear much more rational and in command of affairs than it sometimes seems from an outside viewpoint they really are? All these points can be acknowledged without serious effect upon the method. We are not claiming that an account is a verisimilitudinous description of the antecedents of action on each and every occasion. Ethogenics is not introspection under another name. Rather we suppose that in both accounts and in actions, the same knowledge of what is socially potent and proper is revealed. It is only in the long run that a match gradually emerges between what is seen to happen and what is said to happen. But however that may be, we take it as axiomatic that unless it can be established to the contrary, the best authorities as to what went on are the actors themselves. Their meanings and their rules have priority in the scientific analysis of the phenomena. To say that they have priority is not to say that they have absolute hegemony over all other accounts at all other times, but rather that as a practical technique they are the accounts from which one's initial hypotheses as to what is happening must be taken. And even in the very last analysis, those participant accounts must not be entirely lost sight of.

The Form and Content of Accounts: Analysis

An account is a discourse generally concerned with some particular social occasion. It is a commentary upon the action on that occasion, dealing with the problem of how it should be interpreted, speculating on the motives, intentions and characters of those involved, and generally offering some kind of criticism and justification of whatever are taken to be the goings-on. We believe that accounts, like actions, are manifestations of individual systems of knowledge and belief about the social world and the actions proper to develop and sustain it. So our schema for representing that knowledge should be reflected in the concepts in accordance with which we analyse actual accounts.

So far as we have been able to see people need to be able to identify those social situations which are distinct in their culture. To be able to do this they must have *tacit* knowledge of the characteristics which mark off each type of situation they can identify. 'Situations' in this sense, become the prime analytical devices. Once they have been picked out from an account as recognized as distinct by the participating informants, other material can be sorted into categories with respect to them. Reference to our theory as outlined in an earlier section of this chapter would suggest that the next most important item to be isolated in an account is the set of rules regarded as operative in each distinct situation. There will be rules of interpretation and rules of action. Most individual actors do not rely upon their own judgment of whether they are doing well in the action, but refer to certain members whose real or even fancied reactions are taken as the expression of binding judgments of propriety. Finally, one must look for some representation in accounts of the personal style deemed appropriate in an encounter in a given type of situation. The persona a person presents and the character he acquires in the eyes of the others drives primarily, we believe, not so much from what he does, but from how he does it. Action is spoken of by use of verbs, style by the use of adverbs. Style may crystallize into persona and persona be understood as a public presentation of a particular type of social being. We shall find all these features clearly exemplified in the talk that accounts for the action on the terraces and that makes what happened in school meaningful and right.

How Far Our Studies Fulfil the Methodological Ideal

Our two main fields of study do not fulfil the methodology equally well. In the study of football fans we have access to the manifestations of action on and around the ground and even a permanent record of some of this action in the form of video and audio recordings. Complementary to that record we have the accounts given by those fans of those very occasions and others like them. Such accounts can be renegotiated, and indeed have been the subject of much discussion between the fans and ourselves. But in the study of occasions of violence in school, only one of our parallel sources can be recorded and studied, namely the accounts, since we were not there when it all happened. Indeed, we could not be there, since we have neither access to the classrooms where 'disorder' rules, nor if we had would social life reconstitute itself as it existed before the camera, tape recorders and people accountable as social scientists were upon the scene. All we have are accounts, and in that part of the study our contrasting sources are those within the class and its social order, and those without, including, of course, the teacher unfortunate enough to have to tangle with the kids whose daily life-situation that classroom encompasses. Nor have we been able to reassemble our group of school informants to renegotiate their accounts in the light of other things we know about schoolrooms in particular and young people in general.

Concepts

To bring our participants' social world to life in the kind of detail that is likely to carry conviction we must not just plunge into descriptions of the world of school and football ground, since without the concepts to see it no alternative to the official picture is likely to emerge.

Violence

Concepts, like other natural species, can be threatened with extinction. 'Violence' has lately been in danger. Its meaning has begun to leak away through indiscriminate extensions beyond its original significance, extensions to cases which would normally be distinguished as cases of non-violence. It has been applied to any influence one person may exert upon another, whether in speech or writing, whether by overt physical interference, whether directly in face-to-face confrontation, or anonymously through the links and influences of an institution. An extreme example of such extension can be found in the description of teaching as an act of violence. Sometimes new uses for a well-established term are so strange and mystifying that they refuse to 'take'. This seems to be the case with the extended use of 'violence'. We shall be using the term in the ordinary sense, without, we hope, any fear of being misunderstood. For the more general notion of one person working upon another regardless of the medium of action, we shall retain the ordinary use of the term 'influence'.

For us, then, an act of violence will be an act of *physical interference* with another, whether or not mediated by the use of a weapon. The physical interference need not be sufficiently forceful or well-aimed to result in some form of damage or destruction to a proper part of the victim, though we suppose that a violent action would generally be painful to the recipient.

Violence proper can be direct, involving butting, hitting, shoving, squeezing, pulling, bending, biting, scratching, kicking, and so on. Or it can be mediated by the use of instruments. The distinction between direct and mediated violence is one of importance, not just because of the mechanical advantage achieved by the mediation of acts of violence through instruments of various sorts, but because an intention to act violently can be indicated by the display of the weapons. Similarly, mimicry of the expressions, stance and actions of a truly violent encounter can represent an intention or threat. From there it is an easy step to the setting up of conventions of symbolic violence, in which just the display without the intention to perform the action, can serve a ritual purpose, that is fulfil some other intention than that usually associated with those expressions, stances, shouted insults and so on. For many fans the wearing of Dr Marten boots, and other 'hard' gear, is likely to have that role, that is to be symbolic rather than instrumental.

But violent encounters among human beings are, like other encounters, essentially social. Physical contact alone, however destructive, does not constitute an *act* of violence. The contact becomes an act only if in some way or another it can be provided with a social meaning. This is of even more moment if, instead of acts of real violence, displays of weapons or aborted action-sequences are produced within a ritual framework. To effect a ritual purpose a social interpretation or attribution of meaning must somehow be available. This point leads us to the concept of meaning.

Meaning

Human behaviour enters social reality in so far as it can be given a meaning. How are we to understand this obvious truth? The notion of meaning is exceedingly elusive and complex. We will be working with a simplified form of a total theory of social meaning. The basic formulae upon which we depend are:

1   That actions are interpretations of movements and speeches with respect to what we take to be the intention of the actor in making them.
2   That acts are the social effects of actions.

We can make clear what is meant by saying that the meaning of an action is the social act which the performing of the action brings about, with the help of examples. We, as members of a culture, interpret a light kiss on the cheek as a greeting. In Anglo-Saxon society it is usually confined to greetings between men and women who are socially, but not sexually, intimate. The act is a greeting, the action is a kiss, that is a brushing of the cheek by the lips as an intended action. The act is a social entity; the action is a physical contact interpreted with respect to a certain intention, namely to greet. Thus the intention of the actor is to perform the act, and local knowledge provides him with the means to achieve it. Kissing in this form, as a proper way to greet someone in a certain relation to oneself, is a social convention. The very same act may be performed through very different actions in other cultures. The 'otherness' of an alien culture consists, in part, of there being different conventions linking acts with actions. Hand-shaking, nose-rubbing, and courtly bowing, are among the alternative actions by means of which a greeting can be carried out.

Behind the specific accounts of meaning we offer in this book lies the general theory of Ferdinand de Saussure (1974). His theory was developed for the purpose of giving an account of the way words have meanings, but it can easily be adapted to the task of representing the meanings of actions. Saussurean theory is concerned with both the external relations of meaning and the internal structure of the system of meaningful elements in a language. These he distinguishes as *signifié* and *valeur* respectively. The act accomplished by the performance of a certain action or actions corresponds to the *signifié* of the meaningful element, the action. But to be able to distinguish the action as a meaningful element in a system of such elements we must be able to represent its *valeur*. This is achieved with the setting up of a relational structure between the meaningful elements of the symbolic system.

The first step is to separate out the types of social episode in which a particular social action has a place, for example, the action of shaking hands. The episodes in which that action figures are classified by reference to local conventions as having the force of the performance of this or that social act, such as greeting, betting, leave-taking, and so on. The first dimension of meaning of the handshake as action is the open set of distinct social action-sequences it helps to perform. But in each ceremony alternative devices could have taken the place of the handshake. Some alternatives would preserve the original meaning, others would change it. The presence of a handshake could be thought of as excluding all possible alternatives, that is it excludes kissing, nodding, spitting, etc. To grasp the meaning of a handshake we must not only see it positively as located in a greeting ceremonial, that is in a sequence of actions identified with respect to the social act they accomplish, but we must also see it negatively, as excluding certain alternatives and possibilities of action. This theory is not really as complicated as it sounds. The *valeur* of a socially meaningful item can be represented by means of a three dimensional grid. On the X-axis are arranged the episode types in which that action plays a part; on the Y- and Z-axes the meaning-preserving and meaning-altering alternatives which are excluded by the performing of just that action.

Finally, one must be aware of yet another way in which social actions have meaning. There is the meaning that derives from an association or convention of reference by which an object or an action comes to represent something abstract. This is the way certain entities come to have meaning as religious symbols. The actions of the marriage ceremony not only serve for the accomplishment of the social act of wedding, that is joining in matrimony, but are also said to symbolize 'the mystical union twixt Christ and his Church'. Sometimes an action or object has a meaning in this dimension that is quite arbitrary. But some symbols acquire their additional semantic properties from some characteristic they have as actions or things. A common form of this process is called 'metonymy'. In metonymic use an attribute or necessary adjunct of something is used as a symbolic object in place of the thing itself.

We would like to propose that many of the gestural sequences, both those directed towards the state of play on the football pitch and those occurring in the interactional posturing between rival fans, can be understood metonymically. A clenched fist, a frosty stare or a head-thrust, feet-planted, arms-akimbo posture, being recognizable as proper parts or adjuncts to acts of real violence, can stand in for the real thing in the ritualized 'aggression' to be described in a later chapter of this book. As we shall show in the later sections, a great deal of the activities of the fans can be understood as symbolic activities in the mode of metonymy. These are performances of the detached elements of sequences of actions which would, if carried through seriously, lead to the injury or death of their 'rivals'.

Aggression

Popular, and indeed even professional psychology, has come freely to deploy the concept of aggression in accounts of interactions between human beings. The term has been used in diverse ways. It has been used as a collective noun for the action-sequences in which one person or a group of people direct action upon another, for the abstract concept of such types of action, as in the phrase 'act of aggression', and for the drive or impulse or intention which animates individual people to interfere with or even physically attack others.

We shall take the term in its third sense, as a property of human beings in virtue of which they are prone to direct action upon others in a typically thrusting and imperious way. Aggression then is what is predicated of those who act or intend to act aggressively towards others. But introducing an abstract noun is not the same thing as providing an explanation.

Considerable differences have arisen between those who have tried to show that aggression is a 'natural' human attribute, having its origins in genetic endowment, or something equally inaccessible to self-intervention and control. Ethologists have offered a good deal of cross-cultural evidence, usually in the form of pictures of infants seizing each others' toys and pushing each other about in sandpits, to support the view that the tendency to direct unprovoked action upon another person is at least universal, even though there is nothing in the evidence to suggest a unique origin for the tendency. Tajfel (1972), in a series of studies conducted within the old 'experimentalist' paradigm, examined the tendency of quite accidentally constituted groups to begin to act against each other. The political character of much of this is not hard to discern. Given that the *biogenic* character of aggression is established it does not exculpate other sources of influence, namely social and psychological, from responsibility for the attacks people make upon one another. Both victim and aggressor would be immune from moral judgment; the former for taking whatever social path it was that made him vulnerable and the latter for unleashing his fury, frustrations or whatever, upon the passive recipient of his cruelty and wrath.

Our position is more complicated. We do not wish to deny that the tendency to act aggressively may have a biological basis, that is be related to some heritable feature, and explicable from the point of view of evolutionary advantage. But the social forms that the manifestations of the tendency take are very various and both historically conditioned and culturally determined. In particular we shall show that there is good reason to distinguish ritual aggressive action, made up of elements of symbolic or metonymic violence, from physical violence directed in an aggressive way towards another human being. We shall use the generic term 'aggro'* for ritual manifestations of aggression in symbolic or metonymic violence.

Order

Public interpretations of the 'unseemly' episodes of life in school and on the terraces are readily available in the popular press. 'Classroom chaos' and 'Fans run riot' will do to typify many hundreds of headlines. Such headlines both raise the issue of order in school and at the ground, and explicitly propose that it does not exist. Riots and chaos are essentially disorderly. Their presence contrasts with the order which might have been expected to prevail but which they have somehow displaced.

To understand the force of these interpretations of what has been happening we must be clear as to what the contrasting but implicit concept of order is supposed to comprise. Order is associated with regularity and uniformity, that is with repetitions of the same or similar elements. Thus a timetable which represents the week by week similarity of the arrangement of kinds of work in the day is a representation of order. A non-uniform irregular disposition of work units from one day to the next would be disorderly. In so far as a timetable can be thought of as functioning like a rule it can be thought of as an instrument of order.

In general in human contexts orderly behaviour has other features than just regularity. In particular it seems to be required to be quiet, stable and relatively slow. In an orderly procession, or an orderly leaving of the ground, the initial sequence of people is preserved, there is no passing and repassing, or quickening or slowing of pace. Similarly, the breaking off from one task, routine or

---

* Etymologically 'aggro' is related to 'aggravation' rather than 'aggression', but the coincidence is convenient.

project, while it is still uncompleted, and the taking up of another, which is itself broken off, unfinished, to return sometimes to the first task, sometimes to yet another, has all the marks of disorder. The extreme form of this sort of thing is random or chaotic behaviour when no project is more than half begun before it is abandoned.

Finally, it seems also to be a taken-for-granted principle that in human affairs where there is order there is something corresponding to a rule to be looked for in the background of the actions which appear as orderly. Rule-following is the typical mode of action by which the structure of the content of the rule is reproduced in the actions of the people, though we may have to explain their aims or the acts they intend, in other ways. It follows from the association of order with regularity (and rule) that there is a close connection between the perception that a sequence is orderly and the expectation that it will continue to manifest that sequential property. From a psychological point of view a good test for orderliness is the degree to which the unexpected does not happen, that expectations are fulfilled.

2
Trouble in School

In this chapter we are concerned to explore the interpretation and genesis of disorder and violence in the schoolroom from the point of view of the pupils. We are concerned with disorder as it is seen by our participants and as it is represented in their accounts. There is no way of telling how many of the episodes described are elaborations produced to impress, or how far they are accurate descriptions of action sequences on which both teachers and pupils would agree. Our interest, however, lies in the principles employed by the pupils themselves to fit the actions they describe into a meaningful framework.

'Trouble in school' has been characterized by 'officials' in the situation as meaningless. As we have seen earlier (p. 5), Tim Devlin's teacher conjured up a disorderly, senseless situation. Order for her did not exist but was something she wanted to impose on the class. But as we will see, order of quite another kind does exist in the classroom, and if we want to understand schools and schooling, a comprehensive account must include both sides of the coin. As we will show, the reality revealed in the pupils' speech is very different from the reality that has often been reported in the media.

It is a central tenet of the ethogenic approach that what seems to be one and only one institution may be embedded in more than one theory, and what may seem to be common and even co-ordinated practices may differ very widely indeed. School is just such an institution. The 'official' theory of schooling, complete with its own rhetoric and its own implicit social and psychological theories is challenged by an 'unofficial' counterpart, such as the one which emerges from our participants' accounts. The unofficial theory is revealed not only in the accounts by pupils of perceived offences against them by teachers, but is also seen in other images of school.

An example of this is shown in what has been called the 'Colditz Bicycle Game'. In schools where this game is played, the school staff are called by the names of the officers and guards of the camp, the exits of the school are named after escape routes from Colditz Castle and they are treated as such when the pupils bicycle out of school. Television series such as 'Colditz' and 'Planet of the Apes', serve as a ready source of knowledge for the conventions of their games and in them we see the deployment of a rhetoric from which the pupils' associated theory of schooling can be inferred.

The Social Context

Schoolrooms are in schools and schools are in communities. Although the links and influences of one upon the other are far from clear, it is not irrelevant to an understanding of the accounts to know how the pupils represent the character of their community. Our participants lived on a large 1960s council estate on the out-skirts of a county town and the schoolrooms they describe were in the local comprehensive school situated on the estate. Their community is geographically well defined. Its social character seems equally so, at least in the talk of our participants. Here is one boy's interpretation of that character:

'You learn to scrounge [here]. Anybody's a good scrounger around here.'
'Why?'
'Everyone's so down in the dumps and poor. Other than that they spend their money too quick. Then they scrounge. It's generally just a couple of bob here or a cigarette or something like that.'
'How can you scrounge if everyone else is?'
'Ah, well, see, it all depends. They might have something one day and you cadge it off them, and you got something another day and they cadge it off you. It's just like a big circle. Or I get it off our old lady. I scrounged a pound off her tonight. I'll have to pay it back Friday.'
'She doesn't give you money when you want?'
'No. Have to work for that. It's hard graft getting it out of her. I have to promise I'll give it her back. Takes me about an hour to get it out of her. She hasn't got enough to go round really. We only get a certain amount a week off our dad [parents separated] and that's about it – and what I take home.'

'What about social security?'
'No, we don't get any social security but we got a rent rebate.
We only pay about £3.00 a week but we get a lot of food, and
an electricity bill, and H.P. on certain things like the fridge
and the telly. It all mounts up.'
'Are there any people who aren't poor around here?'
'Oh yes. Our next door neighbour's pretty rich. He's a
photographer. He's on about £10,000 now. Not bad for an
estate house. Not all of them are. I don't know why some are.
They're all drunks around this place. You go in the pub, you
see hundreds of people in there all night. They spend their
money too quick. Have luxuries they can't afford, like me.'

We were told the area was a pretty dull place. Typically they said
things like:

'Generally, it's a bore. There's not much to do around here.'
'Oh, I'm a bit bored with the area because there's not
much to do. If you haven't got any money it's tough. Nights
when clubs aren't on or discos aren't on you get bored. If
you've got money you don't. You can go in a pub and have a
chat with your mates.'

Boredom featured strongly in their account and even the local
youth club, which they went to frequently, was not valued very
highly. As one of them said,

'See, this place in here, I hate it. So does everybody in here.
They hate it, but it's like a magnet. It draws you in. It's
somewhere to go.'

Not surprisingly, given their perception of the adult social world,
drinking, whether at home when their parents were out, or illegally
in pubs, seemed to make up a large part of their activities. This often
seemed to be taken to excess and getting drunk or 'blind drunk' was
described as common practice, at least within their world as they
revealed it to us.

Our Informants

If we take examination passes or examination aspirations as the
measure, the type of person we are talking about here is the non-
academic pupil. The school is the type that has not adapted itself to
alternative, non-academic needs and which, in general, is not sen-

sitive to the fact that pupils are people with as much right as anyone else to be respected.

In the perception of our non-academic pupils, school is represented as a waste of time. It is not treated as 'serious', that is, as a part of their 'real' lives. In other words, they as pupils are not living fully in accordance with the official school rhetoric. For most of them, officially proposed tasks such as learning seemed to involve highly conventional behaviour fulfilling a ritual, the meaning of which was not apparent to them.

This is not just an arbitrary theory of schooling which they have dreamed up, but derives from their perception that they have been 'written off'. They believe that to those who work within the official theory of school they are non-persons. They had little difficulty in finding abundant evidence for this hypothesis. As one girl said:

> 'The way you were treated by the teachers if you were staying on was a lot different than if you were leaving. They sort of couldn't care less if you were going to leave at the end of the fourth year. All their time was spent on the ones that were going to stay on, so ones that were going to leave at the end of the fourth year were never there and nobody sort of worried about them.'

Skiving was not infrequent – the pupils slipping out once the register had been called – and one boy had a job without officially leaving school. As he said,

> 'Well, I thought if I don't get these exams, I won't get a job, because that's what people rubbed into us, and then I thought, well, Christ, if I went down town now and had a look, I bet there's a dozen jobs that'd suit me. So that's what I did one day and ended up with a job.'

For most of the pupils – of the type now readily labelled 'ROSLA kids' – school is seen as an unpleasant trap and a deterrent to life. They do not fit the conventional academic system in which there is seen to be little alternative provision for their needs, so they opt out altogether from involvement in school and wait resentfully for their official release at 16.

A Schools Council report (1970) has emphasized that the problem is not that this sort of pupil leaves school at the earliest opportunity but that as far as school learning goes they 'leave' at the age of about 12. From then on, the school message is clear. They have become devalued as people in their own right and everything that happens to them subsequently serves to reinforce this impression. In his discussion of educational failure, Creber (1972) makes the following point,

> 'Boredom' is not the worst enemy, nor 'relevance' the best answer. The ultimate inhibitor of learning is that undervaluation of the individual implicit in the traditional tendency for the teacher to notice, above all – and perhaps exclusively – what a child *can't* do.

Couple this with all the marks of ritual degradation and the undermining of dignity and we have a damaging and possibly irreversible social experience. Impressions of the world outside school add to their frustrations. They are prevented from entering what appears to them the more appealing world of work, a world in which they can earn independence and the goods that money can buy. Lack of formal paper qualifications to obtain good jobs is no deterrent at this stage. Regrets come later and the trap is confirmed.

'Messing about': The Basic Sequence

Trouble in school is conceived by the pupils who take part in it both as a natural reaction to being in a classroom confronted by a teacher, and as a specific response to particular offences on the part of the teacher. As we will see shortly, there are a number of specific offences and principles of retribution that emerge from our participants' accounts, but there is also a discernible generic category of action-sequences, namely, 'messing about', or 'dossing about'. This is seen both as a device for testing the seriousness of the teacher and thus his/her attitudes to the pupils themselves, and as a retributive routine for dealing in an orderly fashion with what they construe as insulting or demeaning.

This basic sequence is illustrated in the following extract:

> 'I was in this lesson and two or three of my mates were messing about, and I was sat across the other side of the classroom and someone chucked a piece of chalk at the teacher and then started shouting his mouth off. Straightaway the teacher "knew" who it was [unjust accusation]. He turned round and kicked me out of the classroom for doing it. So I hit him.'

Any action by the teacher which is deemed an offence is retaliated against without question. From the pupils' perspective they are not there to accept passively any offensive action on the part of the teachers merely because they are pupils. Of course, what it is to 'be a pupil' is in some ways just what is at issue all along. Our participants had the clear perception that they also have powers within the classroom, conceived as a specific social setting, and they act to establish themselves and their powers. This is done, it seems, not so much to exercise their powers *per se*, but to counterbalance the perceived affronts to their dignity.

This basic sequence often appears in a more elaborate episode structure in which an element of provocation is added to the sequence of offence-retribution. So, for example, a teacher who had already manifested an inability to 'control' a class, will have this failure taken as an insult by the pupils and this weakness will be played on by further messing around which is designed to explore its extent, ratify the insult and perpetuate the cycle.

The Recognition of Offence

In the previous section we identified a basic sequence from which 'trouble' emerges as a cycle of offence and retribution, elaborated in later phases to include a secondary cycle based upon past occasions of offence. In the secondary cycle the offensive stance or attitude of someone, usually the teacher, has to be reconfirmed, so to speak. The new sequence begins with a provocation which, if well directed, generates a new offence from the provoked teacher. The new offence becomes the occasion for another and now legitimized act of retribution. In an effort to understand the psychological bases of these cycles, we can begin by taking each stage separately. We begin with a study of the categories of offence.

For all our participants, and undoubtedly for many of this age-group, a central issue that is constantly recurring in their interpretation of the day-to-day practices they encounter in their social lives is the extent to which they are recognized as persons of independent dignity and standing. They are consequently highly sensitive to any occurrence that might offend against this principle. We found that many of the school practices were interpreted in this way and an expression of the general basis of this contemptuous type of offence is found in the following comment.

'We were still treated as kids when we were in the third year, well, we still are.'

But why is this so sensitive an issue at just this point in their lives? We believe the answer can be found in the idea of a 'moral career'. As we defined this in Chapter 1, a moral career is the temporal trajectory of public reputation and self-esteem, and their opposites. At about the age of most of our participants the moral career of a child with its childish criteria of worth comes to an end. Then one's moral career as an adult begins. The tests and hazards are different, and perhaps have yet to be encountered. In the world of adults a 15-year-old usually has little or no reputation. We would suggest that the extreme sensitivity to self that characterizes adolescents is not just a psychological phenomena, but a social one to be understood in terms of moral career. This is essentially a social concept since it represents the social development of a person, that is of the concept of self in the eyes of others.

Offences of Contempt

1   *Teachers Who Are 'a Load of Rubbish'.*   Teachers who were arrogant and distant fell into this category and it is easy to see how they offend against the central principle and are deemed contemptuous. Two typical comments along these lines are as follows:

> 'Mostly . . . they're all straitlaced. Keep putting us down.'
> 'They go on as if they were never young and did the things we do.'

Less obvious is the offence by those teachers who are unable to break out of a strict interpretation of their teaching role, that is, as purveyors of information and nothing else. As one of them said,

> 'There's a few teachers who you can get on with and talk to. They seem to understand you. But most of the others, it's a nine-to-four job. After that, forget it. [They] Don't pay any attention, just do what you got to do and get out as quick as you can.'

This appears to be interpreted as an offence of contempt from two standpoints. First, in the classroom the teacher is giving recognition to only a part of themselves, and a failing one at that when he concentrates on schoolwork. Second, if the teacher dashes off as soon as school is over (s)he cannot care about it and so (s)he cannot care about the pupils who attend the school.

From the good teacher, pleasure and respect is derived. Such a teacher is marked by the way in which the pupils are treated seriously, no matter how frivolous the content of the interaction.

'He's old, but he understands people.'
'He sort of treated you like, well, he didn't treat you like a
pupil. He treated you as one of them. He'd knock you about
and swear at you and everything, but, you know, he makes
you feel sort of more at home.'

'He talked to us, yes, but he wouldn't lecture us. He'd talk it
out with us and get it settled. For instance, if you were given,
say, poetry, and you couldn't get on with it, he wouldn't sort
of force you into it, he'd sort of talk it over and find out why
you didn't like it, couldn't get on with it, and then he'd put
you on to something else you did like . . . That's the only
teacher I've found that would sort of give you variations of
English, different sides to it. He was like one of us, you know.
I mean, if you'd been talking to him during the lesson he'd
say, well, if you want to talk about it, leave it till after the
lesson. I mean, we used to talk about anything to him. Mostly
he always used to take the mickey out of the girls because
they always used to talk about their boy-friends and what they
were doing on different nights and that, because you see,
most of them went out with boys from the same school, see,
and he knew them. He used to sort of let the girls know what
they'd been at. Mind you, he used to tell the boys about the
girls as well. Mostly they're not like him.'

2 *Anonymity.*   One's sense of oneself as a person is closely bound
up with one's name. A later volume in this series will explore the
social psychology of names in greater detail, but for the purpose of
this chapter we need to draw only on commonsense understanding
of the importance of names.

Not surprisingly, one potent source of offence, interpreted within
the framework of practices which depersonalize and are therefore
contemptuous, was the failure of the Headteacher to know people's
names. Adults gradually come to recognize and forgive name-
aphasia, probably as they come to experience it more and more
themselves. Not so our participants who treat the inability of someone to remember their name as an act of personal contempt. Couple
this with lies about recognition and the offence is great. As one girl
said of her Headmaster,

'You can go in there and he'll say, "Oh yes" and try to think
of your name. He doesn't know who you are but he'll say he
knows you. He doesn't know any individual apart from the
ones that are in there every day.'

3   *The 'Soft' Teacher.*   Each new teacher is put through a period of what we can call social apprenticeship by the pupils in order to ascertain what sort of person and disciplinarian (s)he is going to be. As one of them said, 'Because he was new we used to play him up at first, until we found out what he was really like.' Being a soft teacher was seen to be one of the worst categories of offence. The pupils are insulted by weakness on the part of those in authority who they expect to be strong and this weakness, once established, provokes more playing up:

'I remember once we knocked one out, Miss Wright. Nobody liked her and, well, we used to play on her because we knew she was soft. She was always crying and storming out of the classroom. And it was a French lesson, I think. Nobody liked French, I don't think. Anyway, she went out to get some text books, so there was a few of us who thought we'd have a bit of a laugh, do something to catch her out. So we got a pair of football boots and some books and wedged them on the door, thinking that she'd naturally see them. She walked straight in. They knocked her clean out . . . there was a big line of us outside the Headmaster's office.'

Like many matters, this form of offence is based upon a perceived contrast. 'Softness' contrasts with expected strength. As we read our participants' accounts, the severity of retribution is to be understood against a background of the degree to which they feel let down in relation to their expectations of those they feel they should respect.

In the following extract we see that an equally offensive act is one in which a soft teacher tries to assert authority, but when challenged gives in. The teacher is condemned, not for trying to be strong, but for being unsuccessful in her attempt to reassert authority:

'She tried kicking me out of the classroom. I'd been mucking around and none of my mates like that. They just started getting mad with her and chucking wooden dice that size at her, trying to hit her, and blackboard rubbers, smashing up the lightbulbs and everything, and in the end she just went in the store-cupboard, crying, so we locked her in.'

We will see later on in the chapter that the way in which this offence is perceived is strongly linked with the pupils' own well-articulated theories about the nature and social value of discipline.

Offences of Unfairness

The pupils reported several different forms of unfairness but the first two to follow are perceived as the most striking in terms of devaluation.

Sibling comparison was considered highly offensive. This involved a teacher treating a pupil in a manner which suggested that he or she was the same sort of person as an older brother or sister who had either offended in some way or was being offered as a worthy model.

> 'I get on well with some teachers. Other teachers got it in for me because my brother went there before me . . . He was a troublemaker and now they're taking it out on me.'

A potential source of an unfair offence stemmed from the pupils' position as 'pupils' as opposed to 'teachers' where, by definition, teachers hold the ultimate authority. As such, pupils often felt themselves 'put down' and 'picked on'.

> 'For a start, I bet they did it when they were our age. I bet they did it worse than us if the truth was known. I said to Mr Price, "Did you skive?" and he said, "Yes, on and off", so . . .'

> 'On my report they write that I'm a bit too chatty, that I talk too much to everybody, friends and teachers. One comment on it said, I talk to the teacher, that is good. Well, I'm the one who gets everyone else going – it starts the discussion. And another comment was that I tend to wear the teacher's patience talking. So I said to them, "Well, if I didn't talk you'd say I was withdrawn," and they didn't know how to answer that. It's true.'

> 'He said something that made the implication that I'd copied and I was sort of so choked I didn't answer. If I look back on that [first year], that was one thing that really hurt me. He meant it. He almost said it, that I'd copied.'

Moving from the theme of devaluation, the last reported example of unfairness involves unjust punishment. Within the official school framework there are penalties for inappropriate behaviour and the pupils acknowledge, at least, its theoretical structure. But what they find intolerable is that penalties unrelated to the 'offence' should be imposed. This merely adds to their already strong sense of the senseless. Witness the following extract:

'The worst teacher I ever knew was the chemistry teacher. I couldn't stand chemistry anyway, couldn't understand it at all, the atoms and the neutrons and all that. I was just lost. And he used to sort of ask you questions you know, sort of sit there and pick on you and if he knew you didn't have the faintest idea what he was going on about he'd ask you all the more, see, and if you couldn't answer it, he used to come up to you, look at you, wouldn't say nothing, give you this funny look and tell you to get in the next room. He used to shut you in the next room and give you a pile of books and you'd have to take notes from about seven or eight different books. His favourite was the telephone directory – all the Smiths or all the Joneses.'
'Oh, not related to chemistry?'
'No, you'd do that for about three or four days and then he'd decide to ask you the same question again just to see if you did look it up.'

The Nature and Social Value of Order

To appreciate fully the origin of these offences we must look more closely at the kind of theories held by the pupils. Where order is concerned, it appears that teachers are disrespected not only for not meting out appropriate punishment when deserved (within the official theory), but also for not exercising discipline within the classroom. But what does this mean? If they don't respond to the control which Tim Devlin's type of teacher wished to impose, what do they mean by discipline?

Apparently, this involves two aspects. First, it concerns creating just the right atmosphere in the classroom for learning to take place at all in a human way. As described in the following quote, the classical silent classroom is made redundant,

'Well, if you don't talk, well, it's just like a funeral. You just sit there, writing. You got to have a bit of fun, chatter, otherwise it makes school boring.'

A balance between freedom, natural behaviour and complete rigidity in the classroom was seen to be the ideal goal. As one of them said, 'You know, you want someone who's pretty strict but who'll let you feel a bit free.' Unfortunately, in this respect our participants had little first-hand knowledge of teachers who provided such a balance.

Second, the instrumental aspect of order is valued so that people who want to can 'get on'. As one of them said,

> 'The people that probably helped me fail my geography, they've left . . . well, they made a continual noise, stopped progress, you know. The teacher had to stop to quieten them down.'

Our non-academic pupils however, were not too concerned about this aspect, but as will be seen from a later section, lack of order was a real problem for those people who wanted to get on and pass exams but were in mixed-ability groups.

So far we have been concerned with the expected actions of teachers in the classroom. But what of the Head? Instead of finding there a source of order which their theories would lead them to expect, they are shocked and insulted to find yet another example of lack of strength.

> 'Yes, Miss Brown. She caught me once when I was drunk in school. Oh, quite a long time ago. It must have been just before I left home in November. I'd been over the pub at dinnertime. I'd bought two bottles of cider and I went down my friend's house and I had two neat vodkas and two vodka-and-limes and I got drunk. And in the first lesson nobody noticed and yet I was really noisy, and in the second lesson nobody noticed. Then in the third one I had Miss Brown. It was the last lesson of the day and I couldn't help it, but I come out with a big burp in the middle of the lesson and she goes, "Fay, are you feeling all right?" and I says, "Yes Miss, of course I am", and then she goes to me when I did it again, "FAY!" and I goes, "It's all right", I goes, "Pardon me, Miss. I'll be all right in a minute", and then she goes, 'I'll let you off this time", and then I did it again – a really loud one, and she goes, "Fay, you're going to have to go to the Headmistress", she goes . . . [At which point her friend in the interview interjects indignantly, "all for burping!"] And she sent me down to the Headmistress and she says, "You've been drinking, haven't you? What have you been drinking?" I told her and she goes, "Where did you get it?" and I goes, "From the off-licence". I wouldn't tell her that I got it from my friend, half of it, anyway. She said, "Well, I hope you have a headache in the morning", that's all she said, and "I'll have to tell your parents". So she sent a

letter home and my dad said, "Yes, well, you'd better not do it any more". I said, "All right, fair enough". And that was all of it.'

The same girl described another incident of this nature:

'You can say anything to her [the Headmistress]. She told me once to do some lines and I goes, "It's not worth you telling me to do them, because I won't do them", and she goes, "Well, I think you should do them", and I goes, "Well, I'm not going to, so I don't know what you'll have to do with me". She goes, "Well, I agree with you that you're an awkward child", and she goes, "Go back to your lesson and do your lesson well". That was it.'

We might expect to find a source of order and sense of confidence in the home, but for these particular people this was just not so. Expectations had at one time run high, but a parallel case of offence by weakness emerged from the accounts of the home. We see the father who fails to meet his expected role as protector and confidant regarded as indifferent and uncaring:

'I don't like my dad very much. I gets on all right with him but I don't like him. He's not like a father as you'd sort of think of a father. Well, they're supposed to be protective, aren't they? He's not. He couldn't care less what I do as long as he knows where I am. I mean, you know, if I said I was going to an orgy he'd say, "Oh, all right, as long as I know where you are". He couldn't care less what I got up to. All he wants to know is where I'm going. And he won't talk to me about Paul [boyfriend].'

We see a son who is quite taken aback that his father does not exercise the sort of discipline he should do:

'I must have been 13. I was coming home from school, smoking, right. I was walking along with my girl and I see my old man and I was scared, you know, smoking, but at the same time I didn't want to throw it away because my girl was there, you know, and she'd see it, and I just kept on walking and my old man stopped and said to me, "Give me a light", and I give him a light, and he said, "I'm away to the shops", and I was, you know, thinking, I can get away with this. I was smoking and he didn't say nothing to me, see.'

Finally, we see the expression of contempt when a father tries to re-assert his authority but backs down after a challenge:

'Well, I had an argument with my father tonight. He said to me "You hardly stay in ever! You haven't stayed in for about two months", which is true really. I'm always going out. I haven't stayed in for about two months, about eight weeks, not one night, and he goes, "I think you should stay in at least one", and I goes, "If you think I'm staying in then you get lost, because I'm not staying in this flaming house", and he goes, "You're staying when I tell you to", and I goes, "I won't", and I walked out and came back ten minutes later and said, "I'm going out, all right?" and he goes, "Okay", and he give me some money to go out and come up here [to the youth club]. So it's really all right. He's under my thumb really.'

The parallels between the structure of disappointment, devaluation as persons, and the cycles of offence and retribution in the home and school are very close.

Gradually, through such experiences, these people find there is no official source of order in two of the social worlds they know the best, school and home. As we are beginning to see, however, these people generate their own rules for ordering their lives, they do not just exist in the middle of chaos. The classroom gives us one example of this, and as we will reveal, one of the places where some form of serious life can be lived is on the football terraces.

Offences Which Are Recognized as 'Legitimate'

It appears from the accounts that quite a different reading is given to occasions of physical or verbal reprimand which fall within the acknowledged framework of official penalties. They are perceived as legitimate, not just because of this, but more importantly because the pupils feel able to respond in the same vein and at the same level. However unpleasant the offence, it remains within a non-demeaning framework. As we will see, offences of this kind are dealt with without hesitation on the basis of simple reciprocity.

Principles of Retribution

Offences are not allowed to pass without retribution. The underlying rule-structure which determines the form that this takes is dependent on how the offence has been perceived, that is, whether it is taken to be demeaning or non-demeaning. Where the offence occurs within a legitimate framework, a principle of simple reciprocity frequently applies. One gives back whatever one has received. As one girl puts it,

'And if they turn nasty, well, we can turn nasty too.'

Verbal insult is returned for verbal insult and on being hit one hits back. In the accounts of classroom confrontation we found no instances of girls resorting to physical abuse, although it was a different matter in the home. Perhaps in school, no one hit them first.

There is a second form of reciprocity where the reciprocal action does not take the same form as the insult. The value but not the content of the offence is returned. This form of reciprocation is used both for legitimate and contemptuous offences. So, for example, we see the pupils messing around, 'to get back at the teachers for telling them off and putting them in detention,' or using physical violence after being unjustly accused of a misdemeanour, or being given a 'soft' teacher.

Simple return of contempt for contempt is hard to manage. It is an advanced social skill. Undoubtedly, this is why our participants often resort to the second form of reciprocation when dealing with offences of a demeaning nature. However, the accounts do reveal the operation of a different form of response in these instances, expressed in what we have called a principle of equilibration. What we mean by this is that when the pupils feel themselves put down, treated without 'seriousness', they behave in such a way as to restore themselves to the status of mature beings. Their conception of dignity then defines the form of their response. In talking about such occasions, our participants describe themselves as making non-demeaning withdrawals into silence.

The teacher whose inability to control the class has been construed as demeaning, is infuriated all the more by tactics such as these. As we see, from the following quote, this has the further effect of humiliating the teacher and leading to *his* loss of dignity:

Fay: 'Mr Potts, he was ever such a laugh: but when he got in a temper he used to really shout and nobody took any notice.'
Rosie: 'Yes, his face used to go beetroot. He stood on the table in one lesson and went like this, "grrr!" We just laughed. He looked so stupid.'

While equilibration can be achieved by positive action, withdrawal is used to effect a balance at a more profound level. One way of being dignified is to be above it all, to be silent when provoked. And one way of negating other people is to treat them as if they are not there. It is not surprising therefore, to find Tim Devlin quoting the harassed teacher as saying, 'The worst thing they did was to ignore you completely.' Looking at it from the point of view revealed in their rhetoric, the pupils were not ignoring their teacher as such. They were restoring a measure of dignity, conceived to have been taken from them, by withdrawal into injured and strategic silence.

In summary, then, we find the following system at work: offences are of two types, demeaning and non-demeaning. Demeaning offences fall into two broad categories, those which are treated by our participants as part of the generally resented background of personal devaluation, and those which call for specific retribution according to rule. Offences in the second category fall into two classes, exhibition of weakness where strength is expected, and manifestations of loss of dignity. The former are sometimes responded to violently, the latter by a withdrawal into a reciprocal posture, exhibiting a dignity proportional to that lost by the teacher. Non-demeaning offences are dealt with according to a simple *lex talionis*.

The Arbitration of Propriety

In analysing social episodes, ethogenics has suggested that we should take four elements as guidelines. These are (a) the distinct social situation, (b) the persona(s) presented within that situation, (c) the rule structure(s) for the occasion, and (d) the arbiters of correct action within that particular situation. So far we have considered the first three elements. Moving on to the last one, we must ask whose opinions in the classroom setting are crucial in the judgment of what is deemed proper action.

Not unexpectedly for our primary participants, what the teachers seem to think counts for nothing. Where the pupils referred to in the next section are concerned, their teachers seem to play a larger role in the arbitration of proper action. This appears to be the case, first, because the pupils like and respect them as a consequence of the way they themselves are treated and, second, because of their instrumental value.

The dramaturgical metaphor would suggest that we look to the audience for the arbitration of the action, and it is perhaps no surprise that the peer group emerged as crucial in this respect. As one of the boys explained:

'If someone will start it [trouble] I'll join in willingly. The situation demands it, I suppose. You can't very well sit there. You get a whole class of thirty-five people sat round absolutely mucking about, chucking books, ripping up books, everything like that, and the teacher stood out in front of the classroom writing a load of work down on the blackboard – you can't really work. So you got a choice. You either stand up and walk out and go to a different class, or you join in. If you walk out of the class you get called all the names under the sun, "cissy", "poof" and all this crap. So you just join in. Anybody that works in a lesson that you doss about in, that you know you're going to doss about in, that's it, you get called "ponce" and everything.'

The range of abusive words quoted here is not without significance. As we shall point out in describing ritual insults exchanged between groups of football fans, the abusive vocabulary consists of words which can be used to cast doubt upon masculinity. It seems that those who try to live according to the official theory of schooling are subject to the same range of ritual abuse as the fans of another club. Perhaps those who live according to another theory of school see their rejection of the official line as contributing a dash of *machismo* to their public reputation. They certainly choose their abuse so as to indicate to those who do toe the line that they have lost it.

But additionally, and given the enormous importance attached to the equilibration of dignity, not surprisingly, we find reference to a form of self-arbitration, where what they have said and done is judged by reference to their own conceptions of their integrity and dignity, regardless of 'popular' opinion or the arbitration of specific others.

G. H. Mead has suggested that there are two general stages in the development of the self (Mead, 1934). The first stage involves the organization of individual attitudes towards one's self arising out of various relationships, and the second stage, which Mead considers necessary for the full development of self, is constituted by the organization of the attitudes of the social group as a whole and this Mead has called the generalized other.

What Mead is calling the generalized other and its effects, can be read as nothing more than the process of socialization in which any one culture or social groupings' values and norms are internalized. It does not necessarily follow that any individual who has not taken on the attitude of the generalized other is any less complete than the person who has and acts accordingly. It might, of course, mean that that particular person will readily be labelled 'deviant', but it is equally possible that an individual could fully appreciate the attitude(s) of the generalized other and yet choose not to act within its framework. The accounts in hand would seem to favour this alternative suggestion, whether within the narrower confines of school society and the rejection of school rules, or within the wider context of acting against the laws of British society as a whole.

An Alternative View of School

Messing About

By way of contrast we have accounts of 'messing about' from the members of a very different school community. What little 'trouble' there is virtually disappears as the pupils rise up the school, developing a conception of themselves as valued persons within the official framework. Nevertheless, in a markedly more muted way, softness, where strength was expected, provoked 'messing about', just as it did in the cycles of violent retribution described by our other informants.

> 'We made a noise and ignored them. The more meekly they reacted, the more we'd go on. Well, those that could [stop us] did so in the earlier years, so we never played them up again. Those that didn't, that was it for them.'

> 'I think that if you first come and show that you're the boss, then you're O.K., and the children will turn round and like you for it. Later on you can start slacking off, but if you come in and you're all weak and everything else like that, then they'll think, oh, we can play this person up, and that's it, you've had it, you know. You can let children go so far.'

> 'Well, I pushed my weight around, mucked about. Well, I still do actually. I make fun of them, annoy them, have a joke with them. We've had five years here and nothing's really been clamped down on us – we must do this and we must do that. They've asked us, but either we do or we don't. We just joke with them. We take the mickey out of Mr Brown quite a lot, actually. About the most out of him. I think we're a handful for them actually, a lot of us. Mr Brown said he really couldn't wish for a more destructive class. Everybody played him up. I was amazed he coped, actually.'

Although playing the teacher up was considered part and parcel of school, the proposition was qualified. They felt that playing around was 'worse in the third and fourth forms, not so bad in the fifth year', and that unruly pupils were 'not in the O level group'. As one of them said,

> 'Well, you see, the thing is, there are very few people in our class or any group I'm in [O level] that seem to go in for playing up the teachers, but I know that in some other classes there are. They sort of lock teachers in rooms and things like that, but it never seems to happen in our class.'

'Messing about' is still seen as a test, just as our first group of informants saw it. But for the members of these schoolroom societies it is a test within the framework of the official conception of school. In short, they see themselves as putting the teachers to an academic more than to a social test.

> 'In the younger years there's more than in older years, I think you'll find. We're more sort of settled down, matured more, I think. There's playing up the teacher but it's more trying to get the better of him or her. I suppose it helps both, doesn't it, really, because if you're trying to catch the teacher out, that means you've got to know your lesson pretty well, because otherwise if you try to catch the teacher out and yet you've been proved wrong, you've had it really. For the teacher it's quite easy just to snap back at you and the teacher's always on his guard, and so I suppose his lessons are more accurate that way.'

For the O level people and those who just wanted to work, mucking around was seen to be unfair both to them because it held them back and to the teachers: here they interpret 'mucking about' wholly within the official theory of schooling.

> 'They seem to think they're there to punish the people. They're there to teach. If you don't want to listen, get out.'

> 'One of the teachers did get played up when she first came here. I think she was a bit soft, you know. There were some boys that really did play up. They had been notified for it anyway, you know. You look at that boy and you think, "Well, he plays up," that kind of thing, you know.'
> *'What sort of person is that?'*
> 'Well, one of them that caused the trouble, he hasn't got a father, you see, so therefore . . . and he was mucking about

and she told him to get out and of course he answered her
back, which I don't think she could take really. Well, she
went and got the Deputy Head and she was a bit upset about
it, and then after that our biology group was chopped right
down, more or less cut in half, and most of the boys went
somewhere else to do their biology while the rest of us stayed
with that teacher and we got on a lot better then, you know.
We got a lot more work done then.'
'Would you prefer that to be the general way?'
'Yes, I think so, because in some classes you get the person
who thinks, well, I'm not going to try. I'm not going to
bother, but there again you've got a mixed class anyway.
You've got people that want to get on and you've got people
that don't want to, you know. So the ones that don't want to
can be left to go somewhere else and let the other ones get
on, otherwise they're going to hold the others back.'

No doubt there is an underlife, but it exists independently of the
officially sanctioned 'career trajectories'. Here pupils and teachers
share a version of the official theory in accordance with which the
pupils can see themselves as valued persons. Not only do they share
the official theory of schooling but they hold ideas about discipline
and order that are markedly more 'traditional' than those they
believe the staff hold.
  Our informants had a well-articulated theory of the relation
between 'work-in-school' and success in a life career that allowed
them to see work-in-school as the first rung of their adult moral
careers. Here lies the sharpest contrast with our other informants,
who treated 'work-in-school' as irrelevant to the gaining of an adult
reputation. How different a picture is conjured up by this remark:

'I used to mess about in the third and fourth forms, but now I
don't . . . I'm leaving school soon and I want to get a fairly
good report, you know.'

Our second group believed their families to be highly supportive
of their official careers in school. And they knew that they had
acquired their theories of the relation between schooling and life
from their parents. 'I've been brought up to think that schoolwork
comes first, you know, if you want to get anywhere.'
  In addition, they experienced a school atmosphere close to their
expressed ideal. As one of them said,

'It's funny – it's not funny, strange. It's a very happy school,
sort of thing. The teachers have a very good relationship with

the kids, you know. There's the odd few that don't get on with the teachers. I seem to get on with most of the teachers in the school, so do most of the other kids. It's like a big family, sort of thing. Everybody knows everybody else, and we all get on well. Some of the organization's a bit nutty. It doesn't seem to work all the time, but that can't be avoided, you know. It's the number of kids you've got, and all the less teachers you've got, you know.'

They also had the considered advantage of being the first-year intake in a new school,

'You got a lot of responsibility. A lot is expected of you, but I think there's more advantages than disadvantages. I think it encourages people. You want to achieve what people expect of you.'

Bad Teachers

It can hardly be said that anything very surprising emerges in the pupils' criticism of teachers. But there are some fairly clearcut points that are worth emphasizing.
1   *General Failings.*   The theme of personal recognition emerges again. Even a teacher who can at least teach is thoroughly disapproved of in the absence of personal relationships.

'I think the teachers who just come here to teach are the worst, you know. They just teach their subject and that's it. They don't want to know you at any other time . . . but most of them aren't like that here. If you're just another person in the classroom then you don't get on half as well.'

Then there are those we can all remember from our own schooldays who just can't teach at all, though we are unable to recall from our own experience any example of the stratagem reported by one of our informants.

'He knows a lot about chemistry, but he's hopeless teaching. He just can't put it forward, so you have to get a book and do it yourself, and then I ask for the syllabus so I can make sure I've done everything. He said, "You're useless, you needn't bother to turn up to the exams", because he thinks I'm going to fail. I said, "You haven't seen my work for the past year, have you?" He said, "No, because you haven't done any."

Well, he hasn't actually collected any in and I've been doing a
lot of work at home for it, you know, masses. So I really was
confident I was going to pass, and he said, "I'll give you a
pound if you pass," which isn't really that good a way of
teaching. He used to tell me I was going to fail but I did so
much work at home it was my best subject. He's just a useless
teacher and he doesn't make me feel really confident.'
'How did you do?'
'I did every one.'

2 *Specific Failings.*   The feeling that a teacher has no real interest in the people in his care need not derive only from indifference.
It may come from their perception that he does not take their ideas
seriously.

'Some of them got up my nose a bit . . . right sods the lot of
them . . . there's a collection of them, the Technical Drawing
staff. They're all little gods. They've all got their ideas, their
philosophies of life. Actually, one bloke . . . he goes on and
on about what life's for. Every lesson his ideas change. He
just gets carried away. He's very boring. There's nothing for
him to do, is there? He just gives us an exercise out of the
book, and he just sits . . . he always seems to be writing
something.'
*'Is it the fact that he rambles on that bores you, or the fact that
you don't want to talk about what life's about?'*
'The fact that he goes on and he thinks his ideas are *the* ideas.
He goes on about his experience of life and how he knows
more about it. I suppose he does, but I wish he wouldn't go
on about it.'

Good Teachers

The most striking feature of pupil descriptions of what it is to be
a good teacher is the great emphasis placed on interpersonal respect.
This is not to be confused with a condescending adoption of pupil
style, which they are quick to read as false (even when it is a genuine
identification).

'Yes, I think the teachers we've got, you know, are very
friendly. A lot of them treat you more as a sort of friend and
an equal rather than looking down . . . there's a few teachers
who treat you like a child rather than like themselves, but
most of them are very friendly . . . well, I think it's mainly

because they're younger teachers ... and there's not such a great age gap, you know. There's not such a great gap in our ideas as well, I think.'

'Wishing to accept us. There's one teacher, he seems to have had a personal interest in each one of us for five years. He knows us all by name, of course, and he's interested in each of us, which is something.'

The respect in which the Headmaster of our second school is held again contrasts with the contempt and even hatred felt for the man who headed our first – the man who didn't know their names.

'He's pretty strict, but quite friendly. He's quite nice. He takes an interest in you, which helps.'

The arbitration of right action is again much more open to influence from the world of adults and, in particular, teachers. They seem to play a larger role in the arbitration of proper action, and this appears to be the case, first, because they like and respect them as a consequence of the way they themselves are treated, and second, because of their instrumental value.

Again, like the others, what they do and say is significantly determined by a form of self-arbitration. Actions are judged by reference to their own conceptions of dignity and integrity, regardless of other influences.

Associated Theories of Discipline

We have remarked already on the 'traditional' case of pupil theories of school discipline. This comes out very strongly in the discussions of life in their school. Although they expressed a great liking for the friendly, relaxed atmosphere of their school, they were, nevertheless, critical that it was often too lax. This viewpoint was reinforced by the observations of those pupils who had attended grammar schools for a while and found the 'stuffy' regimes distasteful and unnatural restrictions an impediment to happiness and progress in the classroom. The difficulty of hitting a balance between total rigidity and disciplined freedom was recognized, but was seen to be an essential aim.

'You've got to decide whether it's ... freer atmosphere and rowdyism or silence and total obedience, because I don't think you ... have any feelings towards somebody in schools

where you just have to sit in silence in sort of neat rows. . . . I
don't think that helps, quite honestly. But there's also the
problem that you lose respect if they allow you to get away
with too much.'

'A good teacher is someone who'll take a good joke but will
make us work to get the work done. We had an English
teacher like that actually. He let us muck around but we had
to get the work in at the end of the week.'

'The teachers get cross and they don't do anything. I mean,
they don't seem to have the power of punishment, so it
doesn't stop. There's no discipline. Well, if there was, people
would learn something . . . a bit more.'

'Well, if I do an essay I like it to be marked. Whereas if the
teacher just doesn't mark it, just gives a comment, or just
ticks it, I tend to get lazy. But if you can see it written down,
you got that for an essay, it's so much better.'

'I've certainly enjoyed my time here. I think it could be
stricter actually. It's an unusual thing to say, but I think
probably if it was strict, it'd get better results. They're not so
strict doing actual work, and those sort of things, I think.
Probably I could have done quite a bit better if I'd been
forced to work, because if I'm not, I'm not so bothered to do
the work. It depends on the teacher, I think, a lot.'

'They don't tell you what to do too much, especially in the
fifth year. I think that is a good thing. I think on some points
they are a bit too easy with us, with people sort of skiving. If
you don't turn up, that's that, they don't do anything more
about it. I think they should try and do something more
positive to curb that sort of thing.'

'You can even cheek your teachers and some of them just
don't do anything, you know. I don't think you should be able
to do that . . . I like it (the school) better, but it's not
strict. . . .'

'I think I'd rather stay here because it's fixed now, but I don't
really like comprehensive schools that much. You don't really
learn much. It's so free. Traditional schools you got
everything formal and systematic. Here you just do nothing
really unless you want to, you know. There's no sort of

tradition to it, is there? It's just like a matchbox, isn't it?'
'But it hasn't put you off?'
'No. But a lot of other people don't do much work. You got a
lot of people slacking up because there's no real punishment
. . . there's a lot of people in this school what would have
worked if they'd been pushed.'

'It's going down, the atmosphere of the school, as we have
more staff of, if you don't mind me saying it, lower calibre.
Because in the first and second and in the third year we had
very good staff who took a pride in the school. You've got the
original ones . . . who still have a caring for the school, but
the newer teachers . . . they've got no caring for it and there's
no consistency in the school.'
'What's a measure of caring?'
'One which – in some lessons you can get away with blue
murder. I think that should be stopped – blue murder,
vandalism and the lot. Now certain teachers can control it and
keep their rooms clean and tidy. I think it's their attitude
because with Mr Price we get away with so much and then he
says, no, and we have a real good old time. While Mr Lamb's
far more subtle. Like when we're doing geography, we don't
seem to be working, but when we started revising we ended up
in two years with seven books, which is goodness knows how
much compared with chemistry or a subject like that. Subtle
control – you get the work done, everybody's happy and you
don't realize you're getting the work done.'

'The teachers, I suppose, are very good actually. They spend a
lot of time and also they're pretty broad-minded. They're
pretty lenient, although there are too many diverse rules.
There ought to be a few strict rules which are obeyed to the
letter.'
'Rules such as?'
'Hard to say, really, you know. I suppose commonsense rules
more than anything. You can't go round splashing paint on
the walls, things like that really. The rules ought to be laid
down based on common sense, not like one-way systems,
things like that. I think they're silly because they just
encourage people to break them. But if you stick to
commonsense rules which you're brought up to believe, or
most people are, then I think it would work better, because
you're in a sort of rules – in the same environment. . . . There
is a system, or there was a system, I don't know whether
there is now, of house representatives and form

representatives which can confer directly to the Headmaster
about rules. The only problem with that is that it's not
necessarily going to be accepted. And unless you're on the
council you can't go there and state your case, you've got to
go through someone else, who maybe doesn't understand it or
doesn't have feeling in it, and so it just doesn't work really.'
*'Do you ever feel frustrated that your opinions aren't being,
listened to?'*
'Well, not really, because you realize that it's got to be. You
can't have 1050 dictators. You've got to have set leaders and
I suppose it could be better, but it would mean an awful lot of
work, wouldn't it?'

Out of School

What other lives can be lived? School seems to offer both our
groups of informants very little in the way of opportunities alternative to those formulated in the official theory of educational
establishments. A large suburban school is too open an institution
for there to be much of an underlife in which to acquire reputation
and to develop an alternative moral career. The underlife must be
lived elsewhere. Various possibilities present themselves to an
active lad. Jock has chosen a life of crime within which to fashion a
self.

With the help of defiant stances and some actual fighting, Jock
establishes himself in public reputation as the kind of tough lad he
enjoys being taken to be.

Here Jock is recounting a moment in his moral career. Notice
how central is his concern for public reputation.

'They go like that, "You're mad, you know. All you Scotch
guys are mad." That used to make me feel good, but it don't
make me feel good now. If they said I was mad it used to
make me feel good. Say, like in X-town two weeks ago. Me
and my mates were there. Me and this little kid of 12. I was
standing with him, you know, and two mates were there with
their birds and I couldn't because I was with this wee guy of
12, watching him, and those fourteen guys got round me and
wanted to fight with me. "You're the big mouth from ——."
And I said I didn't want a fight. And I was walking away, and
turned and gave him a great kick, you know, right in his balls,
and I said, "Come on then", took a mad fit, you know, and I
was stone cold sober. I says, "Right, come on then." And as
soon as everybody down —— found out, they go like that,

"Oh, come on then", you know, started saying it every time they see me, you know. Saying I was mad and all that. It used to make me feel good, but it don't any more.'

In Borstal the maintenance of the 'tough' style calls for a different presentational technique, a sustained, harsh, abrasive and un-yielding confrontation.

'And I goes in to this guy, and he goes like that, "Hello, sit down." And I said, "No thanks, I prefer to stand", you know. That's the way I turned when I went in the jail. Turned deaf. If anybody wanted to help me, be nice to me, I didn't accept it. It was just the officers and the screws, not the boys, the boys was O.K. But it was just I turned as soon as I went in, right, as soon as they wanted to be helpful, right, a copper would go like that, "You no got a fag, son?" "No." They'd say, "Do you smoke, son?" Then they'd go, "Do you want a fag?" and I'd go, "Stuff it up your fucking jack", or something like that, see.'

But Jock has seen that other 'careers' are available to someone with a good command of himself. The career of paranoid psychotic attracts him, particularly as a way of coping with the inevitable consequence of his defiant style of living the criminal life. His knowledge of the presentational requirements of the public per-formances demanded of that dramaturgical role is extensive. He has derived it from his observation of his father.

'Well, see, he's a paranoid, you know what that is. Paranoid psychosis.'
'Paranoid about anything in particular, or doesn't it make any difference?'
'Well, you know, like he says he was coming up to you – this is the way I look at it – coming up to ask you to lend, say, a lawnmower, right – this is when he's no drunk, ordinary sober, you know – and he'll be walking up to you and thinking about it at the same time. What if she don't give me a loan of it, what if she tells me, you know, "eff off," or something, and by the time you come to the door, he'll go like that, "Just keep the lawnmower", you know what I mean. He thinks too much. He's in hospital right now. He'll go in for about four months, they'll give him shock treatment and all that, but as soon as he comes out he starts drinking again. He don't try!
'I'm going to tell you what I'm thinking of doing. I haven't

told anybody, right, so I want to tell somebody to see what they think of it. Listen to this. This is a good thing. See, my old man, he was going off his nut, right. My mum went to the doctor and says to the doctor. "My old man's going off his head, you know. Fighting and all that. Doing stupid things like walking round the tables and counting all the time and things like that." And the doctor went up to see the old man and got him put in a hospital and that, in a mental hospital, for six weeks, right. And this is what I'm thinking of doing, so don't laugh at me, because I'm thinking of doing it. No, listen. I'm thinking of telling my mum what I done and telling her to go to the doctor and tell the doctor that I'm doing stupid things and that, to get me put away. Do you think it would work?'

'*Well, it might get you to a psychiatrist.*'

'Because I was under psychiatric report. In the jail – for aggression fits. See, all my records are of aggression, assault, serious assaults, actual assaults.'

Jock's choice emerges as a lonely and demanding life. But Shirley, Bill, Keith and Roger have found a more comradely social milieu in which to begin their pursuit of the good life, and to seek out occasions for the establishment of a reputation – Football!

Questioner: And what about school?

Bill: I'm never there.

Shirley: [sarcastically] I love school – best days of my life.

Questioner: Why do you think that Saturdays and football is better than school?

Shirley: 'Cos it is. You can come up and let yourself go – shout about and that and muck about. Where we live and go to school you can't do that.

Roger: You can get it out of your system . . . get rid of your frustrations about your parents and that.

Bill: You can let yourself go.

Roger: They get on your nerves.

John: You haven't got teachers – they ain't up at football. They're not on your back and telling you what to do all the time.

Keith: Yeah – they always tell you what to do. But that doesn't happen at football. You're on your own – you're free. They ain't in the ground.

Roger: One of our teachers – Mr P—, he's here.

Questioner: Does he support Oxford United like you?

Roger: Yeah – but it's all right 'cos he still can't do anything if he sees us mucking about.

3
Life on the Terraces

Territory

Young supporters at every football league ground (and at many non-league grounds) have defined sections of the terracing as their own territory – an area from which they always watch the football game. Although, to the casual observer, the terraces may seem unremarkable slabs of tiered concrete, certain areas within them are sacrosanct to the fans who habitually occupy them. The chosen section is usually in the open areas behind the goals – areas of the ground which have traditionally been occupied by working-class men since the grounds were built. Such areas also tend to be the cheapest to get into. These territories are known by the generic term *Ends* and each ground has a distinctive name for its End. The 'Kop' of Liverpool and the 'Shed' of Chelsea are two well-known examples. In addition, many Ends are known by the name of the road which runs past the turnstile entrance to them – eg. the 'Stretford End' at Manchester United and the 'London Road End' at Oxford.

Ends such as these are reserved by the home fans solely for their own use – visiting fans being relegated to other areas of the ground. These 'away' areas are often behind the opposite goal to the home End and are recognized by the visiting supporters as their 'spots'.

The distinctive nature of Ends is further reinforced by the subsequent actions of club officials and police. Once territories have been established by young fans, occupants are physically confined within them for the entire duration of the match. Barriers have been erected at all Football League grounds in the light of recommendations made in the Lang Report (1969) – their purpose being 'the segregation of young people from other spectators'. In most cases this has meant that steel fences and wire grilles have been built around the Ends and the areas most frequently occupied by young visiting supporters. At some grounds (notably Manchester United's) security fencing and iron grilles of the type that zoo cages are made of have been installed.

Young fans, particularly those wearing what we shall describe as the standard 'Aggro Outfit', are directed by the police and officials into the appropriate secure area of the ground as they enter. Both the police and the fans themselves refer to this process as 'penning'. Persistent attempts by fans to get out of such areas and into the opposition's area is one of the most common reasons for their arrest or ejection from the ground.

In addition to these measures, fans are further restricted by 'dry moats' dug between the terraces and the pitch itself and by suitably dispersed groups of 'trouble shooting' police constables. Many grounds also employ Alsatian dogs around the perimeter of the pitch, and police spotters are often to be found with binoculars and two-way radios in the TV camera gantries below the roofs of the main stands. At Leeds United's ground the system of control and restraint has reached perhaps the ultimate in sophistication. Here senior police officers sit in a windowless room, facing a bank of video-monitors and operating, by remote control, TV cameras which can zoom in on any area of the terraces or stands.

The net effect of the fortifications around Ends, and of the strategies to keep people in them, is, of course, the highlighting of their distinctive nature. The police and officials have succeeded in delineating fans' territories in a way that the fans themselves could never have done. Another by-product of official strategy is one which involves the fans and the police acting in a concerted and co-operative manner. The maintenance of territorial integrity has become a joint enterprise. Invading fans are not only repulsed by the occupants in defence of their home 'turf', but also by the police in their pursuit of law and order and the *status quo*. It thus comes as little surprise to find that police and fans share similar commonsense conceptions of territoriality, and that their accounts of what goes on during 'raids' on Ends have much in common.

The notion of territoriality here is quite critical to an understanding of social action on the terraces and to the social structures that exist. Territories here are seen as action-facilitating in the sense that many of the patterns of action we have observed rely for their appropriateness on the fully defined context in which they take place. Using the notion provided by Erving Goffman (1971), and further elaborated by Lyman and Scott (1970) football Ends are viewed as 'free' territories. As Lyman and Scott explain:

Free territory is carved out of space and affords the opportunities for idiosyncrasy and identity. Central to the manifestation of these opportunities are boundary creation and enclosure. This is because activities that run counter to expected norms need seclusion or invisibility to permit unsanctioned performance, and because the peculiar identities are sometimes impossible to realise in the absense of the appropriate setting. Thus the opportunities for freedom and action – with respect to normatively discrepant behaviour and maintenance of specific identities – are intimately connected with the ability to attach boundaries to space and to command access to or exclusion from territories.

The free territories of the Ends become 'converted', through regular use, into 'home' territories. A special kind of relationship comes to exist between users of such a territory and the physical space itself such that new conceptual and linguistic markers are attached to the space. Unlike most forms of home territory, however, Ends are not colonized in opposition to authority. In reality, the guardians of authority collude in the maintenance of the territory once it has been colonized, and as a result enter into the social framework on the terraces. Police at football matches are not seen as the immediate enemy in the way that they might be, say, in dealing with trespassers or others laying false claim to an essentially public area. They may be seen as obstructive when restraining rival groups of fans, but the venom and anger characteristic of, for instance, thwarted political demonstrators, is noticeably absent at most football matches.

During the 1974 and 1975 seasons young supporters of Oxford United were concentrated in an area of terracing known as the 'London Road End'. During the close season in 1974 a dry moat had been constructed and new barriers installed. The setting in some ways was a little unusual in that rival fans occupied the other half of the same block of terracing. In 1974 the two rival groups were separated by a corridor of barriers patrolled by police. In 1975 a steel fence was added on the visiting supporters' side of the corridor to further restrict access between the two halves. Figure 2 shows the general layout at Oxford United. The home fans occupy the left half of the London Road end.

Most football grounds now divide their rival fans by placing them at opposite ends of the ground and by preventing access between the ends. At Leeds, for example, not only are fans separated in this way, but a wedge-shaped piece of terracing at the corner of the visiting fans' terrace is designated a 'no-man's-land', surrounded by high fencing, and kept empty. Any fan trying to get from one end to the other would have to pass through this area and would be

immediately arrested. Strategies at other grounds are often even
more elaborate. With the Oxford system, however, a distinct inter-
face existed between the two sets of rival fans, and although kept
apart by police and fences, it was still possible to 'get at' the

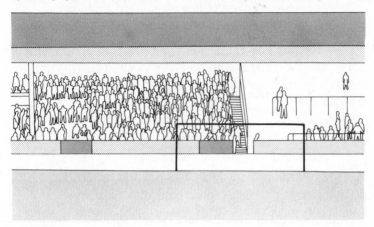

Figure 2

opposition with determined effort. The system also resulted in
chants and songs being directed sideways to the rival fans, rather
than across the pitch to the other end.

The fact that visiting supporters were allowed in to the same
terracing, even though distinctly segregated, was a constant source
of irritation to many Oxford fans, and it was often pointed to as an
explanation for the occurrence of 'bovver'. The label 'London
Road End' was carefully used to refer only to the half of the terrace
occupied by Oxford fans.

Social Groupings at Oxford United

Initial research work at Oxford United's ground consisted mainly of
making a large number of video-recordings of fans in the London
Road End. These were made discreetly with the aid of a telephoto
lens and with the full co-operation of the club. Early analysis of
these tapes revealed a grouping pattern in the London Road End
which remained quite static over a considerable period of time.
Later reports from the fans themselves revealed that they were very
aware of such groupings and were able to attribute a number of
salient behavioural and social characteristics to them. The main
groupings are shown in Figure 3.

Group A comprised boys mainly between the ages of 12 and 17. The mean age of a sample of thirty-four boys in this group who were to contribute greatly to the later stages of the research was 15·1 years. The most distinctive aspect of this group was the pattern of

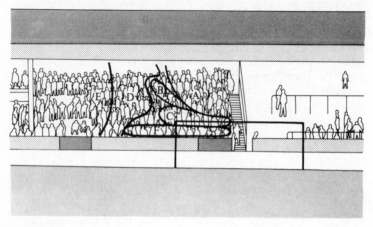

Figure 3

dress – the 'Aggro Outfit' which is discussed in Chapter 4. The presence of flags, banners and emblems of allegiance was also very marked. When the newspapers and television hold forth about football hooligans it is usually to members of groups like this that they are referring. Not only are they the most identifiable group in terms of their appearance, but also in terms of the high level of activity among the group which is apparent even to the casual observer. They make the most noise – singing, chanting and shouting imprecations against the opposition fans – they run the most and they can represent a rather awesome spectacle to their rivals. For this reason we refer to this group as the *Rowdies*, rather than the media appellation of hooligans, for as we shall see, the label 'hooligan' carries special meaning within the soccer micro-culture.

Group C, in contrast to the Rowdies group, consisted of rather older boys and young men up to the age of about 25. The mean age of a sample of fourteen was 18·7. The style of dress within this group was unremarkable and differed little from that worn by people of this age group in most social contexts. Nor were any banners or flags visible. In fact, members of this group would not be identifiable as football fans at all outside of the ground. Younger fans referred to this group as the 'Town Boys' and were clearly deferential to them.

Group B, lying between the Rowdies and the Town Boys on the right-hand side of the London Road Terrace, was a much less distinct group which varied in composition from game to game. One consistent characteristic, however, was the presence of a disproportionately high number of boys with a record of arrests, probation and care orders. Out of a total of seventeen boys from this group interviewed over a period of one year, no fewer than ten had been in trouble with the police for offences not connected with activities at football matches. This compares with an overall average of about 8 per cent for the London Road End as a whole.

Apart from this characteristic, the group seemed to have features of both the Rowdies and the Town Boys groups. The average age was about 16·5 and some of the more distinctive dress elements were present. The activity level, however, was much lower than that of the Rowdies and some of the fans in this group were only infrequent attenders at football matches.

Groups D and E were much less homogeneous than any of the others and effectively marked the edges of the active arena in the London Road End with which we are concerned. In the main, they both consisted of boys and young men who were rather more reluctant to join in the ritual chanting and singing and were even less keen to get mixed up in the aggro. The only difference between the groups was that those in E were generally a little older and a few females were also to be found there. Both groups contained a number of fans who were scathingly referred to as 'part-time' supporters by those in the Rowdies and the Town Boys groups. Among such part-timers were a few public-school boys playing at being football fans but failing really to understand what it was all about. The left-hand boundaries of these groups was totally undefined.

In group F were to be found young children (average age about 10) who sat, when they were not moved off by the police, on the wall in the front of the terrace, overlooking the dry moat. Their major occupation consisted of watching the antics of those at the back in the Rowdies group. Because of the age and inexperience of these boys, we refer to this group as the 'Novices'. Other fans simply call them little kids, but they are to be distinguished from other 'little kids' in other areas of the ground.

The pattern of grouping described here is probably unique to Oxford United's ground, but analogues of such groups appear to be present at all league club grounds – with the possible exception of some of the very small Fourth Division grounds. What is most striking about such groupings is that they provide for *careers* on the football terraces. The Novices, Rowdies and Town Boys provide a fairly linear hierarchy. Fans may aspire to progress through this hierarchy, and within each group certain role positions are open. The role positions enable demonstrations of character and worth, leading to the attainment of status, to take place within an ordered and rule-governed framework. 'Becoming somebody' on the terraces is a highly structured affair, and an understanding of this structure is the first step in rendering the apparently anomic behaviour at football matches intelligible.

Careers

In using the by no means original sociological concept of 'careers' we do not wish to imply that action of the part of soccer fans is somehow *determined* by a restricting set of institutional restraints. We would certainly want to use the term 'careers' in a rather different way from some criminologists who speak of 'delinquent careers' in which young deviants are inescapably forced along the path of community school, borstal and prison. Rather we see careers in a much less mechanistic way – as available structures in a youth culture for the establishment of self. At this point we are seeking only to explain the social frameworks which render certain actions intelligible, and we do not wish to imply causal links between social frames and social action. The extent to which fans will carve out careers for themselves on the terraces will, to a large extent, reflect their commitment to the soccer culture and to their immediate peer group. The greater the commitment, the more a fan has at stake. But, as we shall see, the richness of the soccer social world provides for commitments to be expressed in many different ways.

We have suggested that the Novices–Rowdies–Town Boys groups provide a distinct hierarchical framework for careers. Such a framework has more than a passing similarity with the career structure observed by Howard Parker in his study of young delinquents in Liverpool. Although his groups, 'Tiddlers', 'Ritz', and 'Boys', reflected increasing involvement in delinquent activities, they served the same function of enabling young people to achieve the sort of reputations and images denied them in mainstream society. On the football terrace, however, the other groups mentioned serve as side channels to the main career framework. They provide for the less committed who still wish to enjoy some of the fruits of the soccer culture. Groups D and E can certainly be seen to have this function. A fan who was totally uncommitted to the culture, who simply wanted to watch the match, would probably choose not to go into the London Road End at all but rather to one of the quieter side terraces. Group B, on the other hand, seems a little anomalous. To some extent we see members of this group as 'failures' in the career development process. They occupy fringe positions to both the Rowdies and Town Boys but have status in neither. Their high delinquency level also puts them at a further distance. But more will be said of this 'delinquent fringe' later.

In charting the progress of fans' careers, two types of data have been used. The first, and the easiest to collect, consisted of biographical material obtained from samples of fans in each of the groups, with special attention given to the Rowdies and Town Boys. The second type of data was obtained from close observation of the changes in the compositions of the groups and in the holders of clearly defined role positions within the groups. Both types of data, however, are problematic in that the whole structure within which careers are established changes over time. Physical locations of groups, for example, are very much influenced by changes in official club policies regarding the positioning of barriers and turnstiles. At one time, the Club went as far as refusing to allow juveniles a reduced entrance price for the London Road terrace but allowed them half price for other areas. The intention was clearly to deter younger fans from getting into what were viewed as 'trouble spots' and, at the same time, to improve the total gate money a little. (Oxford United is a very impecunious football club.) For a time fans were split. Many remained in the London Road End, but others established a new piece of territory at the other end of the ground where it was cheaper.

Other changes in structure developed more slowly, but although the pattern *looked* different over a period of a few years, analogues of the basic groups seem to have been present ever since the phenomenon of the contemporary football fan arose in the middle to late 1960s. There has always been the equivalent of the Novices group, for example, allowing entrance to the soccer microculture for any boy willing to learn the rules of being a fan. Similarly, the Rowdies have always made their presence felt – as any 'old-timer' will eagerly tell you. At one time the Rowdies were mainly Skinheads for whom the terraces were but one of a number of arenas for collective action. Those most dedicated to soccer culture became known as 'Terrace Terrors', but their successors are currently moving away from the baggy trouser and braces image that they fostered. Rowdies today often have quite elaborately coiffeured hairstyles – contrasting markedly with the heavy Dr Marten footwear which they still retain. Finally, Rowdies have always had the more manly and mature equivalent of the Town Boys to join once they had proved their worth and their masculinity.

In interpreting data, then, the gradual changes in the social framework at Oxford United have been taken into account. Note has also been taken of where particular groups have positioned themselves at various times in their evolution, and of the differences in style which have characterized such groups over time.

Two distinct aspects of the career process are to be distinguished. The first of these, the between-group *graduation* process, is concerned with movement from one group to another and with the fact that membership of a particular group affords a certain status in relation to members of other groups. The second, the within-group *development* process, is concerned with the establishment of certain well-defined status positions within each group and with the acquisition of the appropriate social knowledge to equip a member to 'carry off' the performances required by such roles.

Social Roles

Social roles within each of the groups have been isolated primarily from the accounts given by fans and from prolonged observation in the London Road End. In many cases fans were able to attach labels to certain positions, but in some cases the role was defined only by the range of behaviours required for it. The Rowdies group provided by far the widest range of available roles, and it is with a discussion of these that we start.

Chant Leader

During the 1974 season about six individuals occupied such a position within the group. The role of such a person was simply to initiate songs and chants and to act as 'caller'. The job of a caller is rather like that of a priest who intones, line by line, the words of a prayer and to whom the congregation respond, at each stage, using the appropriate replies. A simple example of this calling takes the following form

Give us an 'O'
[O]
Give us an 'X'
[X]
Give us an 'F'
[F]

etc.

What have we got?
[OXFORD]

At other times the chant leader is required to initiate chants in reply to a chant from the opposition fans. A common example of this occurs in the interposing of an imprecation in between a chant of allegiance by the rival group. Thus, a chant of '*Chelsea!——Chelsea!*' is transformed into *Chelsea (Shit!) Chelsea! (Shit!)*. The job of the chant leader is simply to make sure that '*Shit!*' comes in at exactly the right time. Other examples of these chants are to be found in Chapter 5.

The major characteristic of chant leaders is that they are all quite tall. They can therefore be seen by most of the fans around them, especially when they hold up their arms to indicate that a chant is about to begin. One individual, however, can never be visible to all fans at the back of the terrace, and for this reason more than one chant leader is required.

Achieving this kind of position within the group requires, in addition to being tall, a full knowledge of the entire repertoire of chants and of the occasions on which it is appropriate to use them. To forget the words in the middle of a chant would be most embarrassing. Quite a lot of fans, at one point or another, succeeded in starting off chants and songs, but few could do so consistently. To fail in such a venture, to sing out '*Give us an "O"* ' and get no response, is to lose face and effectively to be deterred from making a similar attempt in the future. To achieve this position a chant leader has to engage in a form of 'hazarding' of a particularly subtle kind.

One might expect that being a chant leader afforded a number of privileges within the group, but this in fact was not the case. 'Leadership' was very restricted to the narrow confines of ritual expression of allegiance and denigration, and carried little weight in other situations. An illustration of this came when the *Daily Mirror*, for reasons of their own, carried a feature article about Oxford United and paid particular attention to Eric – one of the most regular of the chant leaders. Immediately after this, a number of fans complained that to over-emphasize Eric's role was unfair, and that although Eric was respected for his loud voice, stature and chanting ability, he was 'nobody special'. Eric readily agreed with this.

One other major aspect of the chant leader's role is related to the creation of new chants and songs. The vast majority of chants are common to virtually all football grounds, with slight variations. Liverpool supporters would have us believe that they all originate from the Kop, but this is doubtful. One reason for the ubiquity of chants lies in the fact that a large number of fans move around the country to support their team at away games. A rapid and wide-scale communication network is thus provided, and good chants can be taken over from one set of fans and used against a different set the following week. From time to time, however, songs and chants of a completely novel kind are heard. The origins are often to be found by watching and listening to what goes on in the Soccer

Specials – the trains and coaches which fans hire to transport themselves to away games. To fill in the travelling time chant leaders are actively engaged in trying out new versions of old chants or making them up from scratch. Those that meet with approval are then usually tried out on the terraces, and if found to have some power, make their way into the repertoire.

Subjects for new, and often short-lived, chants often reflect 'in-jokes' which, because they are totally unintelligible to the opposition fans, can be used to create confusion among them. On one occasion, for example, a member of the delinquent fringe had arrived on a special coach with a cardboard box containing two gross of packets of Maltesers. In a short space of time, the coach was sticky with chocolate and fans were being sick out of the window. On arrival in Nottingham the chant *'If you all hate Maltesers clap your hands'* had gained considerable currency. Bemused fans of Notts County thought that this was some oblique reference to their West Indian members.

Aggro Leader

An aggro leader is not to be confused with a 'good fighter' for, because of the peculiar nature of aggro,* he might never have to do any fighting at all. At Oxford United a person occupying such a role would have been one of six or seven boys who were always at the front when conflicts arose with the rival fans. In 'running battles' they would always be the last to retreat. For these purposes they would also tend to wear the most heavily reinforced boots and might occasionally carry weapons of some kind.

Within the Rowdies group, there was some confusion as to who was and who was not an aggro leader and also with regard to the characteristic behaviours expected of such a person. Three fans were placed in this category on the basis of lengthy observation and in accord with what were taken to be the appropriate criteria for judging such people. These boys, however, turned out not to be aggro leaders at all. This was because a very important dimension had been ignored – one, which in keeping with everyday social talk, we refer to as 'Bullshit'. In order to prove himself as an aggro leader, a fan has not only to prove his ability to lead charges but also the fact that he really means what he is doing. The manner in which he must

---

* We make a strong distinction between 'aggro' and violence. Aggro we take to indicate a ritualized expression of aggression which, by and large, is not seriously injurious. A full development of this theme is postponed until Chapter 5.

do this however, is not always clear. He may do it by actually 'clobbering' somebody, but this would imply a rather drastic escalation of the conflict situation and happens too rarely for everyone in the aggro-leader role to prove themselves. Instead, there simply has to be some consensus among the Rowdies that if things got really bad he would still maintain his stance and be man enough to deal with it. Evidence for such qualities might come from other areas of youth culture. Thus a boy with a reputation for challenging the authority of his teacher in school, or with a record of resisting the restraints of the police, might find it easier to be accepted in the aggro-leader role. Without a reinforcing reputation he might simply be classed as a 'Bullshitter' – the boy who thinks he's hard but isn't – and rejected accordingly.

Phil, a 17-year-old currently in borstal for a cheque book fraud, and for a time one of the most respected 'hard men' of the London Road End, had these comments to make about his role as an aggro leader:

> 'Lots of the smaller kids really look up to you. Me and Rich – we always get all these kids crowding around us – away matches specially. They look up to you and think you're a good fighter.'
> *'And are you a good fighter?'*
> 'Yes – well me and Rich fight from time to time. Not so much now 'cos they get a bit scared – but used to quite a bit. If people start some trouble or something like that then I'll be in there – but I don't go round looking for it or anything like that. If you live up on the Leys [a local housing estate] then you have to fight or else people piss you about and think you're a bit soft or something. . . . At the football I try to keep out of it. If fans from Millwall or Villa or somewhere like that come down – causing trouble and that, then I'll have a go. I mean, you can't let them come here and think they can walk all over you, because then next time they come they'll get a bit cocky and think they can do what they want. So I'm in there – making them run – that's what you're trying to do – and make them feel small. So we're round outside after the game and down the road after them. But I don't go round thumping people all the time. You don't have to. People know who you are.'

Being in this kind of role clearly affords a great deal of status. In fact aggro leaders are probably afforded the greatest degree of deference within the group and by novices as well. It is this sort of person who is always allowed the best seat on coaches, is given cigarettes, whose suggestions concerning strategies in conflict situations are always most heeded, and who is generally held in the highest esteem. All this may be achieved without recourse to bullying or intimidation. Leadership of this nature seemed to be thrust upon certain members without them having to achieve dominance over would-be contenders for the title.

In general, an aggro leader has to show a distinct sense of fearlessness – he has to be a 'hard case'. But his lack of fear must not be too great, for total fearlessness, the issuing of challenges against impossible odds is the prerogative of the nutter. And fans are in no doubt as to where bravery ends and sheer lunacy begins.

Nutter

There are usually about five or six nutters in the London Road End at any one time. These are individuals whose behaviour is considered to be so outrageous as to fall completely outside the range of actions based on reasons and causes. Typical of their behaviour would be 'going mad', 'going wild' or 'going crazy'. Attempting to beat someone to a pulp would be described in these terms. It is the existence of this kind of role, and the presence of notions of 'unreasoned' action, which is taken as strong corollary evidence for assuming the existence of a tacit awareness among fans of the rules governing social behaviour on the terraces.

To call someone a nutter, however, is not to use what they would see as a term of abuse. It is simply to make a comment about their style of doing things. Blackpool fans even have a chant which runs: *'We are the Nutters – we come from the sea'*. The implication would seem to be that the opposition fans had better watch out because Blackpool fans might not be restricted by normal conventions. The chant *'There's gonna be a Nasty Accident'* probably expresses a similar sentiment.

We talked to nutters frequently over a period of two years and some were 'interviewed' in a more structured manner. All of them were aware of their role and didn't seem to mind too much that their peers thought them to be crazy. They tended, however to be much less articulate than others in the Rowdies group and to possess far less social knowledge. But it would seem that nutters are more accepted among soccer fans than among groups in other areas of youth culture (cf. Paul Corrigan (forthcoming) and Howard Parker (1974). The function of their role we see as being, like that of the deviant in relation to society, the visible demonstration of the limits to 'legitimate' action. The nutter is acceptable in that he demonstrates to other fans what they should not do, and provides living proof of their own propriety. It is at this point that we can begin to see how deviant groups – even evil Folk Devils – construct an order which in many ways is based closely on the order of the society which makes them outcasts.

Although the behaviour of nutters is clearly different from that of other fans in the Rowdies group, there is still a sense of order in what they do. Even 'going crazy' involves the following of certain conventions and restrictions, as we will further elaborate in the next chapter. In many ways, their crazy actions are analogous to the hysteria of young girl pop fans, who on first sight seem to be totally out of control, but can clearly be shown to be engaging in an intentional, conscious and structured activity. (See Marsh 1975.)

Hooligan

The term 'hooligan' derives from the name 'Houlihan', a noticeably anti-social Irish family in nineteenth-century east London. Since 1970, the media in this country have become very attached to the label, judging by the extent to which they increasingly use it. Before this time, fans were referred to mainly as 'ruffians' or 'tearaways' and the use of 'hooligan' marks a distinct stage in the media's contribution to deviancy amplification. But as Laurie Taylor and others have shown (Taylor, 1976), terms which originally begin life as terms of abuse or disapproval often become used by the victims of the term to mean something quite different. Thus football fans have incorporated the term 'hooligan' into their own social talk and use it as a term for referring to boys who commit acts generally thought worthy of some praise. Such acts often involve minor damage to property or disruption of certain routine social events. The main characteristic, however, is not the act itself, but rather the manner in which it is carried out – in particular it has to be funny. Picking up a bubble-gum machine from outside of a shop and running off with it, for example, would be generally thought rather dull. Picking it up and pretending to do a rather elaborate waltz along the road with it, on the other hand, would be thought of as a much more creditable act of hooliganism. The object is not to create damage and disorder *per se*, but to carry out an act which is guaranteed to enrage the victim without doing what he thinks you are doing, i.e. stealing his machine. In all probability the machine would be replaced once the 'laugh' was over, and failure to do so might well lead to censure from others in the Rowdies group. Those most skilled in carrying out such activities and getting away with them come to be recognized within the group as hooligans.

Hooligans have something in common with nutters in that they

both provide the group with a good deal of entertainment. The
hooligan, however, tends to have the longer career since part of his
art lies in knowing how far to 'push his luck'. The nutter, in contrast,
is constantly being caught by the police because part of being 'nutty'
is absence of any real form of self-preservation.

For a whole season at Oxford United, Geoff, a 16-year-old fan,
held the position of a 'right hooligan' and was renowned for his
'wicked' acts. One of his friends gave this description of one of his
typical escapades:

> 'Once, against Swindon a couple of seasons ago, there's this
> fat cunt and Geoff's standing outside the ground before the
> match and this cunt bungs a bit of old dog shit he's found by
> a wall at him and it hits him on the arm. . . . Anyway, at half
> time, Geoff's standing right at the back of the London Road
> – and at the back there you can see down to the tea place
> underneath because some bugger's smashed out some of the
> asbestos bit along the back. Anyway, he sees this fat cunt with
> some of his mates with some tea – and he's moved along a bit
> to the end and he's pissing down and out through the open bit
> and its all blowing down on these cunts' heads and into their
> tea and all over – and its raining a bit as well so they don't
> notice. Me and some others, we run down and were watching
> this and we're killing ourselves. But Geoff, he don't shout out
> or anything – he just waits for a bit till they finish their tea
> and then he shouts out "Enjoy your tea then", and as they
> look up he pisses a bit more and they go barmy.'

This may seem a rather distasteful episode, and it is undoubtedly
more than a little apocryphal. But whether or not it is a completely
accurate report of what actually happened is perhaps not the point.
This is the way hooligans are seen – as perpetrators of the gratuit-
ously outrageous act which nobody else could ever manage to pull
off. Other fans may feel the need to embellish the stories about what
hooligans do, but the embellishments stop short of pure fantasy.
There is always a sense of reality and credibility in the accounts.

All this contrasts markedly with the media image of the hooligan
as a purely destructive agent. To see hooligans as destructive is to
miss the subtlety of their actions – it is, in a sense, to be conned by
the hooligan into believing what he wants us to believe about him.

Becoming a hooligan within the Rowdies group is not a simple
matter. Powers of witty innovation have to be developed which
enable a fan to change the whole nature of a social situation. In a
sense he must be a jester – a player of practical jokes and a bit of a
'devil'. But he must never be simply a 'clown'. Clowns in the social

world of soccer fans, are the pathetic figures who will never make it. They are the ones who aspire to being hooligans but lack the 'bottle' to succeed in such a role.

Organizer

The London Road End always seems to have at least one organizer, and usually two. Their function is simply that of dealing with the business aspects of terrace life and of negotiating with the outside world. Chiefly they are responsible for hiring coaches to away matches and for getting occasional petitions signed. The need to hire coaches arose from the fact the Supporters' Club actively discouraged membership from fans under the age of 18. The Club claimed that this was because the premises were licensed but fans had other interpretations. The effect of this was that young fans rarely got the opportunity to travel on the Supporters' Club coaches and, since travelling by British Rail was often a hazardous and expensive venture, alternative arrangements were needed. Mike, now training to be a chartered accountant, was one of the most efficient and respected organizers the London Road has ever seen. He would book coaches well in advance and collect the fare in instalments prior to each away trip. The fact that he also made a little money for himself in the process was considered only reasonable by the majority of fans. During his time as organizer there were no instances of damage to the coaches, and on every trip a whip-round was arranged for the driver.

Petitions were sometimes drawn up when a need was felt to comment on official club policy. Occasions occurred for this when the manager was sacked and when the admission charges were put up. The petitions had little or no effect but at least they afforded some sense of involvement in what was going on.

Like the other roles we have sketched, being an organizer required a particular set of skills and a particular commitment to the group. It demanded a lot of work and the carrying of a great deal of responsibility. But it provided the occupant of this role with a very central and secure position within the group via a means that required no conflict with the rest of society.

Other social roles within the Rowdies group were much less easy to isolate. The ones described so far probably represent the major positions available to fans, but it is vital to note that simply having a strong relationship with an occupant of one of these role-position holders also afforded some degree of status. Being Phil's mate, for example, was something which many fans aspired to even though they could never hope to carry off the performances required of an aggro leader themselves. Like any group there were, of course, scapegoats and 'creeps', and such individuals inevitably got pushed around and blamed for everything. But what was noticeably absent was any serious intra-group rivalry. Rivalry, when it did occur, was usually deliberately manufactured when the number of visiting fans was too small to constitute any real opposition. Only at these times did any sub-divisions within the Rowdies group become apparent.

The sub-divisions which arose were, in the main, based on where fans lived or went to school. During a very dull match one might hear chants such as '*Berinsfield Boys are Wankers*' or '*Gosford Boys, we are here*' '*Doo da' Doo da*'. Similar patterns could also be observed on the coaches to away matches. Conflicts of a very minor nature were manufactured out of anything. Boys sitting on the right-hand side of the bus, for example, would set up in opposition to the boys on the left in order to have someone to mock and to shout joking imprecations at.

The major purpose in outlining the roles within the Rowdies group has been to demonstrate that football fans of this type are not simply to be viewed as a disordered bunch of maniacs. But a demonstration of orderliness must also involve appeal to an existing social structure which serves to 'institutionalize' action – that is, to impose a set of constraints on behaviour and, at the same time, to endow action with meaning. For this purpose, we need to show that the roles serve as a focus for patterns of social relationships and for a framework enabling social development. With this in mind, one must be concerned with how fans gain admission to the Rowdies group, how they are able to progress socially within the group, and with how they are able to graduate out of the group.

Admission to the Rowdies group can be obtained in one of two ways. The first method involves graduation from the Novices group. Having spent some time as a 'little kid' at the front of the terrace, and having learned through close observation the most rudimentary rules of conduct appropriate to being a Rowdy, the young fan simply shifts his location to the back of the End and to the fringes of the Rowdies group. Here he will have to serve a form of apprenticeship before he is accepted or even noticed. An exception to this might arise if a young fan has, as a Novice, shown special merit which has come to the attention of others. He might for example, have shown himself to be a 'little hard-nut'. A small boy of 8 called Louis had done just this. His diminutive figure was always to be seen during battles with the opposition, and for this reason he gained exceptionally early admission to the Rowdies as a kind of unofficial mascot. Apart from Louis, however, most Novices moved quietly up when they felt ready for it. Within their own group there was little to strive for since there were no clearly identifiable roles available. Nor was there much in the way of a social structure. Novices 'hung around' together but there were few strong ties between them.

The other method of entry to the Rowdies was by joining one's mates from school or local housing estate. In this way many fans were able to miss out the first graduation step and serve a short probation at the back of the terrace. It should be remembered that there are no formal rules for admission to the Rowdies. Anyone who is prepared to wear the right 'gear' and to join in the singing and chanting will be accepted. Identification with the team and engaging in the correct patterns of support for it are sufficient. (So long as one isn't a 'creep' of course.) Having gained admission, the way is then open to choose the direction of one's career and to become known by name to others in the group.

In charting development within the group two samples of boys have been used to reduce the task to manageable proportions. During the 1974 season thirty-four boys were enlisted and the exercise was repeated with a smaller group in the following season. These boys were not chosen at random but on the basis of their being, *a priori*, representative of members of the Rowdies group as a whole. This task was made much easier by Mike, the organizer, who knew everybody and encouraged their co-operation.

Of the thirty-four boys in the first sample, twenty-six had joined the Rowdies group directly by having friends already established within it. The other eight had 'grown' into it from the Novices group or its historical equivalent. About fifteen of the boys said that they felt some need to prove themselves to the others and to become known to them by name. Virtually all the boys in the sample were known by name to at least three others in the group and, in the majority of cases, to considerably more. By piecing together all the interviews, and on the basis of continued observation at matches and elsewhere, a rough approximation of the fairly static social structure is shown in Figure 4.

Although Figure 4 looks like a sociogram it should not be treated as such. Lines linking two individuals represent an indication of association between them, but the nature of the relationships vary. In order to keep the diagram simple only data for the most central twenty boys are included. The sample breaks down into three clear sub-groups, and adding in the other fourteen boys would not change this picture. S1 always stood out as a unit and these boys, who were always together, were known by everybody in the sample. The other two sub-groups were similar, but members within them had little contact with the rest of the sample other than with boys in S1. The distinctive nature of this pattern was best illustrated in the coaches to away matches. S3 always sat at the front, S2 at the back and S1 in the middle. Boys 14 and 15 once tried to sit at the back of the coach but were rapidly sent to the front where, it was said, 'they always sat'. The scapegoat and the remaining members of the group had no fixed seat and sat wherever they could. Similar patterns of dispersal

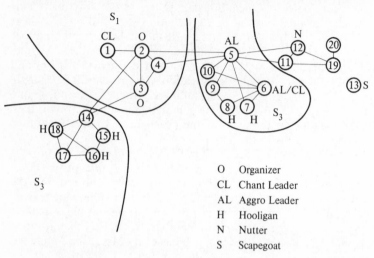

O	Organizer
CL	Chant Leader
AL	Aggro Leader
H	Hooligan
N	Nutter
S	Scapegoat

Figure 4

could be seen on the terraces themselves, with S3 always standing further back than the rest.

This desire for knowing one's place, even at the level of physical location, was very marked within the Rowdies group. Where one stood and where one sat in relation to others was always very prescribed. In many ways it was like the staff common room in a school where institutionalization of this nature always seems to be very strong. There was a similar need to understand one's place in social terms. Fans often described themselves and their position in terms of their relationships with others. They might introduce themselves as being the best mate of a particular fan or as the one who hangs around with a particular group. In describing his social contexts Mark, who was Mike's best mate made the following comments.

'Me and Mike(3) – we always go together – and Martin(1) – the coloured kid too – and John(4) who's at my school as well. We're a kind of little click [clique]. But you get to know lots of others to talk to and that and on trips to away matches then you get to know them a lot better. But Mike and me, well mostly Mike really – he organizes a lot of trips and gets

the buses and coaches and things like that – and we collect
money from the other kids on the Saturday before. . . . But
we're there with everybody really – singing and shouting and
that . . . you're all together and it doesn't matter who else is
there as long as they're Oxford fans . . . it's all about the
team, isn't it? . . . We run down the other end and have a go
at Sunderland fans . . . and like against Villa when they all got
pushed onto the pitch . . . we're all in there. . . . But we don't
go round smashing things up all the time like some kids. Its
more for the excitement really and the football. . . . I started
coming just after Mike came – that was four seasons ago, and
Martin he came two seasons ago and he used to live in the
same street as me.'

One of the aggro leaders, a 16-year-old boy called Rich, also had
interesting things to say about his time in the group and about his
rise to the position he held:

'I've been coming to games at the Manor since I was 10 . . .
not every week like but since three seasons ago I haven't
missed a match – I've been to them all. But it used to be
different then . . . there wasn't no atmosphere like there is
now and there weren't no fence around the London Road like
now. . . . It was about then [three years ago] that I started
going with some of my mates like Kevin(10) and Eddie(6) . . .
and Eddie and me we got into a lot of fights and that . . . and
the fucking coppers – they always grab either him or me when
there's any bother or that. We been in Cowley nick so many
times they keep a special room for us and inside it's got Eddie
and Rich written on the walls – and they don't bother to clean
it off 'cos they know we'll be back and write it up again. . . .
A lot of kids – when there's any bother they all start running.
That's the trouble with Oxford – they run too much. But
Eddie and me and kids like John(8) and Alf(9) we always get
left there. These kids was coming at us once and six of them
grabbed hold of me and when I turned round all the others
had fucked off and left me to get a kicking. . . . But John, he
doesn't care or nothing about how many there are – he'll just
fly at them fucking mad like and have a go. [This John is a
nutter.] I try to keep out of it a lot now but I'm not scared or
nothing. If someone wants to have a go I'll give it to him. But
I wait for him to start it – and then I just finish it off.'

The Rowdies group represents the most salient stage in the fan's
career. It is within this group that he comes to establish both

personal social bonds within his particular sub-group, but also comes to feel part of a wider social collective, as witnessed by the 'we're all in it together' type of accounts given by members. It is also within this group that a fan has the most obvious opportunities for becoming somebody special. By the time he has reached the age of 17 or 18, however, a new decision has to be made. By this time a fan will be working and will be getting too mature to maintain the style of dress and behaviour that membership of the Rowdies group requires. Two choices present themselves. He can either 'retire' to less active parts of the ground (assuming he wishes to continue watching football) or he can seek acceptance with the Town Boys.

The Town Boys in a way are an enigma, and how one joins them is by no means easy to discover. They speak disparagingly of the Rowdies, yet many of them were once Rowdies themselves. They have a reputation for being tough but rarely give any evidence of being so. In fact, at most matches, they do very little at all except set up a few chants when things are a bit quiet. Despite this, however, it was possible to isolate two major roles within the group and to gain some insight concerning the requirements of anyone wishing to graduate into this group.

Fighter

About six members of the Town Boys were consistently referred to as people with reputations for fighting. Stories were told about how they had actually done considerable damage to some visiting fans when situations had got out of hand. There was no indication that they, unlike the aggro leaders, were actively engaged in inciting other fans to join in the scraps or that they led concerted attacks against the opposition. Rather, when trouble had boiled over, which was pretty rare, they were the ones who stood and slugged it out. Two such fighters were persuaded, over several pints of beer, to talk about themselves and the reputations they had acquired. (One doesn't simply *interview* a fighter.) One fighter had been a Skinhead and had worn the appropriate 'gear' of his time but had now grown out of this kind of thing. (He was 22.) The other fighter came from Nottingham four years ago and had seen much worse than one ever saw at Oxford. At Nottingham, he claimed, there had been a tradition once of wearing metal pit helmets at football matches. The peaks of these helmets, however, were sharpened up with the aid of a file and 'nutting' someone whilst wearing such a weapon, he claimed, could literally chop their head off. Both reluctantly agreed that they had reputations for fighting, but insisted that they had not strived for such status. They only fought in order to protect some-body else ('like one of the younger kids who's getting smashed up') but were clearly very capable of making a good job of it. They totally dissociated themselves from the Rowdies, who they thought of as kids, who, by mouthing off all the time, started trouble which was left to them to finish off. One of the fighters later became a club steward, and dressed in a white coat with a red armband was officially hired to sort out the Rowdies.

Heavy Drinker

A number of other young men in the Town Boys group were well known for their ability to drink impossible-sounding quantities of beer. Estimates of the volume varied, but a figure of fifteen pints in one evening was common. Many appeared to be visibly drunk at matches and were often thrown out by the police for this reason. They did, however, provide a good deal of entertainment for the rest of the group and would be missed if they did not turn up for a game.

The common feature of all members of the Town Boys group was that they had all held dominant roles within the Rowdies group or its equivalent at some stage in their careers. Their entry into the Town Boys appeared to rest not only on the fact that they had gained reputations but also on their ability to maintain such repu-tations in the absence of the symbolic dress and tokens of status which had assisted them in the past. An aggro leader, for example, needs a particular set of clothes in order to maintain his image. Simply being 'hard' is not enough. But if he can leave all this behind, and wearing only ordinary casual clothes still keep up his peers' belief in him, then the Town Boys are likely to accept him. Not only will he be accepted on the terraces but also as a drinking partner in the local pubs. Similarly, other Rowdies who have been shown to have given long service through organizing or chant leading might also have a chance of making the grade.

Membership of the Town Boys represents the last promotion in the career of the football fan at Oxford and only the most com-mitted are eligible. Having got this far they can rest on their laurels for as long as they wish. No more will they be called upon to prove themselves by engaging in certain prescribed activities and no longer need they safeguard their hard-won reputations. Eventually they will retire to other parts of the ground to watch the match with their wives and girlfriends.

It would be a mistake to claim too much for the career structure or to suggest that the graduation process is a rigid one. There were many fans who drifted in and out of the groups without making any sequential progress at all and the groups to the left of the terrace always provided for an escape from the soccer 'rat race'. One should also remember that for a period of about three or four months in the summer the terraces are closed completely. Positions and statuses are held in abeyance until the following season until they can be redefined and re-established. It would also be a mistake to suggest that the rhetoric of careers is present as such in the everyday conceptual system of fans. In fact it is not – it is a gloss which we have imposed on the accounts and stories they have provided. But this does not mean that any undue 'stretching' of the data has taken place. On the contrary, some of the best evidence for the presence of a linear graduation process has come from the biographical material given by samples of fans in the three major groups.

In collecting biographical material fans were asked to give accounts of the ways in which they had come to their present position in the terraces and to indicate on a sketch plan of the London Road End, past, and projected future locations. They were also asked to describe the major characteristics of the groups in which they had found themselves at each point in their time on the terraces. Such material was collected in a variety of ways, ranging from formal tape-recorded interviews to casual discussions in and around the football ground.

Information from the Novices showed quite clearly that they all saw themselves as working towards a position at the back of the terrace. When asked why they would make such a move, most replied that

'It's more fun up there.'
'My mates are up there.'
'It's where everyone goes.'

Such a move, however, would rarely be made during the course of a particular season. Instead, the Novice would wait until the start of a new season and, having managed to buy some appropriate clothes, would then 'appear' at the back of the terrace. Observations of the composition of the groups over three seasons confirmed that this was what happened. Many of the Novices also expressed an ambition of 'getting in' with a particular group of individuals in the Rowdies group. From their lowly status they were still able to perceive who was who in the Rowdies hierarchy and which sub-units were worth making a try for. Many, of course, had brothers or older friends in the Rowdies group and had already had some experience of 'hanging around' with them in other social arenas away from the terraces.

Novices who had been in the London Road End for at least a good part of one season displayed quite a detailed acquisition of social knowledge which was appropriate to correct conduct in the Rowdies. Most seemed to know what one should do there in a variety of situations in order to be an accepted member. Those lacking this knowledge tended not to succeed in the first graduation step and usually were to be seen a year or so later in either group D or E.

All of the sample of Rowdies were able to plot very accurately where they had stood on the terraces over the last few years, who they had been with, and where they expected to be in the future. There was a steady shift over time from the edges of the group to positions near the central barrier and towards the front of the group. Most talked about an increasing feeling of security within the group. David, for example, had this to say about the three years he had been in the group:

> 'When I used to come here first of all I didn't know
> everybody like now. I knew some of the kids from school but
> not most of the City kids [he lived in Witney]. But that's the
> thing about football. Because you're all United fans you
> become part of something that's big. Its the atmosphere that
> does it – its electric. Other kids get to know who you are and
> what you're made of. If you show them you're not scared to
> really get in there you make a lot of friends. They know me
> now in the London Road and that's great. They know me and
> Paul and Steve 'cos we've been around here in this bit of the
> London Road for three seasons now and they know that we
> wouldn't let them down.'

With regard to their futures, most of the Rowdies felt that they would 'pack it all in' when they left school or when they were 17 or 18. By 'packing it in' they meant that they would stop wearing the uniform and 'tearing around' so much. Some felt that they had mellowed already and that they weren't so active as they had been before. A few said that they would like to be a 'Towny' or at least be able to command similar respect. None, however, felt that it was possible to 'join' the Town Boys in any simple sense. There was a feeling that the Town Boys were an arrogant elite and to actually get in with them you would probably have to do a lot of serious drinking in the Marlborough Arms. Living outside of Oxford would also be a serious handicap.

The origins of some of the Town Boys have already been mentioned. From the biographical material it was sometimes difficult to chart progress accurately because the groups from which they had graduated were no longer in existence. Many, for example, talked about the gangs they had once been involved in but these gangs, if they remained at all, were not, as one Town Boy said, 'a shadow of what they used to be'.

We have been suggesting that career structures can serve well in the explanation of social behaviour which might otherwise appear to have little rationality. The activities of a fan become intelligible if we can interpret them as being instrumental in establishing him in a particular role, or if such activities can be shown to be acceptable demonstrations of character and worth among his peers. This is not in any way to imply any moral or ethical stance on our part. The task is not one of excusing behaviour or of attributing condemnation to it – only one of rendering it explicable in terms of a revealed social order. We may not like what fans do and we may view aggro leaders and their like as unhappy reminders of a violent society in which we live. Similarly we may see the nutter as a pathetic figure who has to resort to self-humiliation in order to establish an identity for himself. But at the same time, we must pay careful attention to what such young people are actually *doing* rather than to the easy caricatures of them which some seem to prefer. Whilst we may feel that it is unfortunate that such career structures exist at all we might do well to examine our own mechanisms for getting ahead. In doing so, we might, to our discomfort, recognize that football fans are playing a very similar game to the rest of us in society.

The notion of careers is, of course, only one aspect of order on the terraces. It provides the framework for an interpretation of action but the full story is only revealed by an examination of the rules which direct action and which provide for the interpretation of situations. It is to the elaboration of rules that we direct our attention in the next chapter.

4
The Interpretation and Control of Action

The Discovery Procedure

Bearing in mind the few points which have been made so far, it is clear that an examination of the rules within a sub-culture such as exists on the football terraces must proceed within the context of an adequate discovery procedure which enables the requirements imposed by the concept of rule to be satisfied. In effect, this means that a good deal of groundwork is called for before one can begin to ask the kind of question which yields directly the tacit meanings and conventions. One cannot ask a question such as, 'What should one do?' before one has knowledge of language use and the conceptual equipment to make sense of the answer. Consider this short transcript from a tape-recorded interview:

Questioner: What do you do when you put the boot in?
Fan A: You kicks em in the head don't you? . . . Strong boots with metal toe-caps on and that.
Questioner: And what happens then?
[Quizzical look]
Questioner: Well what happens to the guy you've kicked?
Fan A: He's dead.
Fan B: Nah – he's all right – usually anyway.

Now quite clearly, a fan who has been kicked in the head with a steel-capped boot is not going to be 'all right'. Neither is he likely to be dead. Without some way of interpreting these answers the transcript is of no value at all. Indeed, faced with material like this one might be forgiven for returning to the tangible security of apparently more orthodox 'scientific' methods in social psychology. At least an experiment allows one to slot responses neatly into operational categories and produce some numbers. And yet, we maintain, even answers such as these can be made intelligible *in the actors' own terms* once we have built up a picture of what the terms of reference are. We also believe, contrary to the claims of some ethno-methodologists, that such terms of reference involve a stable pattern of ascription of meaning to objects and events – in other words, a rule-like semantics. It is to this end, and ultimately to an appropriate understanding of the rules themselves, that a discovery procedure must lead.

The existence of rules cannot be directly inferred from the observed regularities of conduct. The fact that one might cycle to work every morning will reveal, to an observer, a distinct behavioural regularity, but there is no reason to suppose necessarily that there is a rule which dictates that one *should* ride to work. At best, we can only infer the presence of a permissive rule which states that one *may* cycle to work. On the other hand, there are reasons why the observation of behavioural regularities can form a vital first stage in a rule discovery procedure. First, bearing in mind the criterion of arbitrariness, one needs to be able to specify the potential range of applicability of rules. To do this a knowledge of the external givens of social events is required and this might be achieved through attention to those features and aspects of the situation which are beyond the control of football fans. Second, attention to the observable regularities of behaviour may yield certain hypotheses concerning what the rules might be within the constraints that have been isolated. For example, activities such as going for a cup of tea at the football ground reveal regularity in that they occur only at certain times of the day, but since the tea stall is only open at those times it would be foolish to suggest that the time at which fans drink tea is rule-governed. If however, the tea stall was open all day, but fans went there only at specific times, this might be suggestive of the existence of a 'tea time' convention among fans. This initial stage, then, of a discovery procedure, which is ethological in its methods, allows statements to be made about what is not rule-governed, and hypotheses to be generated concerning what the rules might be.

At Oxford United this initial analysis was conducted with the aid of video-recordings – the method also revealing some of the data on which the initial assessments of social structure were made in Chapter 3. Some comparisons were also made with data collected, in a variety of ways, at other grounds in order to demonstrate that at this level Oxford United was reasonably representative of most other football clubs. On the basis of these data and from information obtained concerning events outside the ground, the invariant sequence of activities shown in Figure 5 was revealed. The most obvious

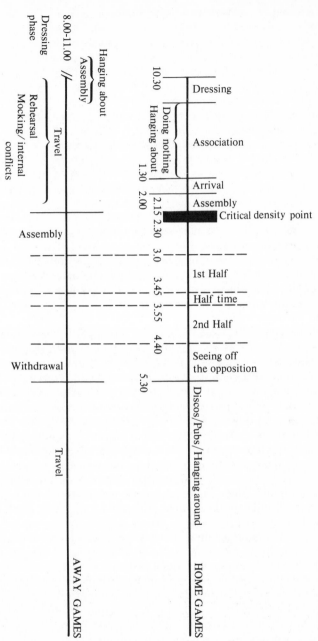

Figure 5

point which emerges from looking at the pattern of activity which occurs every Saturday (or at least when there is a football match) is that the actual game itself serves as a focus for other events which precede it and take place afterwards. For the football fan, and in particular the Rowdy, 'football' lasts from about 11 o'clock in the morning to 6 or later in the evening. Where travelling to away games is involved, an even longer sequence is present. Placing the two sequence patterns side by side gives us a picture of what both groups of rival fans are doing at every football match.

For the home fans the 'preparatory stage begins about 10.30 a.m. with what might be simply referred to as a dressing-up phase. Football fans take their 'gear' very seriously indeed and as we suggest later, much of what they wear has distinct symbolic value. Football gear is special. It is usually only worn on Saturdays and although styles and fashions change from season to season it is always kept up to date. It is selected with reference to current styles and also with reference to a certain impression of one's own character and status that is to be communicated to others. What football fans wear is, in itself, very much rule-governed and these rules are to do not only with the major requirements of fashion but also with what is appropriate gear for one's position within the terrace hierarchy.

The second phase in the preparatory stage can be seen as involving association and assembly. In the case of home games, fans meet their friends in prearranged places and as small groups engage in varied but regular activities. Older fans meet in pubs whilst the younger fans 'hang around' particular locations on the route to the football ground. Even 'hanging around' has a distinct structure to it and what might appear to consist of 'doing nothing' conceals a quite intense activity. [See Paul Corrigan's (forthcoming) study of Sunderland street-corner culture.] Assembly procedures are clearly instrumental in the weekly reaffirmation of social relationships and role positions. Simply by looking at who meets whom and in what order we can begin to get some idea of the sociometric structure of the football fan culture. For away matches the length of the preparatory stage usually depends on the distance to be travelled. On average, coaches leave at about 11 a.m. but this can vary widely.*

---

* At one time special coaches would sometimes leave in the middle of Friday night when long distances had to be travelled, often arriving at 8 or 9 in the morning in the town where the game was to be played. This practice came about because of the law relating to the number of hours a coach driver could spend actually driving and the compulsory rest periods he needed to take. Coaches were hired with only one driver in order to keep the cost down, but this meant that a very long rest period was required

Most fans, however, arrive at the coach departure point well in advance – often up to an hour before the coach is due to leave – and once more 'hang around'. During this period the various sub-groups form up, some sporadic chanting and singing might break out and seats on the coach will be 'booked'.

The coach trip itself provides for a very distinct set of activities, some of which were outlined in the last chapter. Distinct grouping patterns within the coach reflect the stable roles and status positions in the group. Some minor, and often deliberately manufactured conflicts may arise during the journey in which different sub-groups set up in mocking opposition to each other and engage in a highly structured ritual of 'taking the piss'. In many ways the coach trip facilitates a kind of rehearsal for the match to come. Chants and songs of a novel kind are tried out and tested. Words of old songs are sometimes modified to make them appropriate to the impending clash with groups of rival fans. In general, an atmosphere of anticipation and excitement is created during a period when fans need something to look forward to and have time on their hands.

The period immediately prior to the game provides for assembly on the terraces. The small groups who have met earlier arrive at the ground from about 1.30 p.m. onwards and begin to merge with others in the appropriate End. Home fans always arrive much earlier than visiting supporters and Rowdies tend to make a point of getting there first. These are quickly followed by the Novices who stand at some distance from the older boys and appear to do very little except watch closely what is going on – which at this point is also very little. It is not until a 'critical density' of fans is reached that any overt and collective activity can be observed. The actual size of the critical density varies enormously from End to End. At Oxford it appears to be quite small – about a hundred fans, but at clubs such as Manchester United or at Leeds the figure is at least five times greater. Once the figure has been reached songs and chants start to develop some unity and the groups of fans begin to merge into the 'shape' which is characteristic of a particular End. At Oxford this shape takes the form of a right-angled triangle. A rather blunt apex at the triangle occurs just behind the goal and the two right-angled sides are provided by the back of the terrace and the fence which separates Oxford fans from the visitors. At other grounds the shape is often less determined by architectural considerations but is always extremely well defined.

---

before he could take the coach back again. The inevitable problems created by hundreds of tired and irritable fans arriving in a town up to seven hours before the match prompted the Minister for Sport to call for new restrictions regarding football coaches and their times of departure and arrival.

As the number of fans in the home End increases beyond the critical point an increasing unity develops in collective action. Songs become more tuneful, chants develop their characteristic rhythms and hand clapping becomes more staccato. This happens irrespective of whether the visiting fans have arrived in any appreciable number in the ground. If they still haven't arrived by about 2.30 chants such as *'Millwall where are you?'* will be heard, and some of the home Rowdies will actually run around the ground looking for them.

In the normal course of events the arriving groups of away fans build up to constitute a recognizable opposition force soon after 2.30 and a period of about twenty minutes follows in which each side runs through its entire repertoire of chants, songs and traditional styles of imprecations and insults. The arrival of the teams on the pitch at 2.50 heralds a deafening escalation of this process right up to the kick-off. Certain chants, however, are specific to this period. Inevitably the opposing team will be diagnosed as having forwards who are suffering from cerebral palsy and a goalkeeper who is homosexual. In contrast one's own players will be portrayed as 'bionic' or superhuman. During this period a rather unpleasant song is often sung at the opposition fans, and its content is of special interest to those who wish to claim that fans are becoming increasingly alienated from part of their working-class heritage. It runs to the tune of 'In My Liverpool Home':*

'In their (Nottingham) slums,
In their Nottingham slums.
They look in the dustbin for something to eat,
They find a dead cat and they think it's a treat,
In their Nottingham slums.'

A more detailed consideration of the types of insults and imprecations issued during this period is made in Chapter 5.

During the period of the match itself fans are involved in the dual task of spurring their team on to victory and of denigrating both the opposition team and their supporters. The more unified an End and the more numerous the fans, the greater will be the perceived impact of their concerted actions. In the normal course of events the conflict will be limited to exchanges of insults. Even though a thousand or more fans might be chanting with blood-curdling sincerity *'You're gonna get your fucking head kicked in'* there may be little or no physical contact between the rival sets of supporters.

---

* This is one example which lends some support to the thesis that a large proportion of such songs and chants originated from the Kop of Liverpool.

This is not, however, always the case. There are certain matches where special historical factors demand action of a somewhat more drastic kind. Where extreme rivalry exists or an ongoing feud or where there has been a lot of 'needle' in the past, the normal routines will tend to be escalated in favour of increased physical contact with the visiting fans. This is not to suggest that the conflict in such cases is less orderly, or that rules of conduct no longer apply. Rather, the rules themselves will tend to be such that a greater number of attacks on the opposition will be called for.

At many grounds half-time provides the opportunity to 'get at' some of the visiting fans more easily. At Oxford fans are separated on the terraces but have to share the same tea stall at half-time. It is not surprising, therefore, that it is here that some of the most interesting patterns of conflict between rival fans are to be seen. The following is one example of the kinds of small-group confrontations which take place with great regularity at this point in the day.

Four Sheffield fans sit eating crisps on a pile of concrete slabs opposite the tea stall. A number of Oxford Rowdies gradually move over and silently surround them. Taunts and subtle threats are made by the Oxford boys and one of their number moves in closer to lead the antagonism. A Sheffield boy, who so far has been looking steadfastly at the ground in front of him, glances up for an instant at the leading Oxford fan. He is immediately accused of 'staring' and is challenged to stand up and fight. The challenge is ignored. Other Oxford boys now move in closer and become more vocal. The leading Oxford fan continues his taunting and starts to flick the reluctant Sheffield boy's collar and hair. At this point the Sheffield boy leaps up, his face red with anger. Adopting a stance with feet apart and arms outstretched, he faces his opponent. The two stand silently facing each other while the onlookers step back a pace. After what seems to be a very long period of inactivity, an inter-mediary in the form of an older Oxford fan arrives on the scene – in fact, one of the Town Boys. He moves the younger Oxford fan to one side and escorts the Sheffield boy out of the conflict area. The police, having been onlookers themselves up to this point, now grab the Oxford antagonist and push him roughly in the opposite direc-tion. There is an almost audible sigh of relief and everyone returns to watch the second half of the match which has now been in progress for about ten minutes.

At the end of the match the two sets of fans once more have an opportunity for contact with each other as they leave the ground. The extent of these opportunities varies from ground to ground but at Oxford both the home and the away fans share the same exit. At Glasgow Celtic's ground, on the other hand, elaborate provisions for separating fans have been made. When Celtic play Rangers, not only are rival supporters carefully kept apart during the game but exit roads from the ground are barricaded in such a manner as to prevent any contact between them as they leave. This has the added effect of forcing fans (and footsore social psychologists) to make long detours around Glasgow in order to get back to the station.

For most fans, and in particular the Rowdies, the day does not end when the match finishes. A lot of running around takes place as rival fans are chased back to their coaches or to the railway station. Having 'seen off' the visitors in this way, Oxford fans form back into large groups and present a rather incongruous spectacle as they chant their way over the tranquil Magdalen Bridge and into the City. Any stray visiting fans they happen to find still in Oxford will be obliged to make a hasty retreat. Finally, fans will disperse – the main corpus splits up into the small groups that were evident during the initial assembly stage, and some fans will stay in town for other peripheral activities which Saturdays have to offer. Such activities consist of going to discos or pubs or hanging around particular streets. Other fans will simply go home to watch TV.

To describe this sequence of events may be to point out something which is very obvious to many people – especially to those who actually go to football matches from time to time. But it is within the episodes which constitute this sequence of events that the rules for which we are seeking are embedded. We can see, for example, that fights, in the sense of involving physical contact between rival fans, can only occur during certain periods – you can't go and 'bash' the opposition at 1 o'clock in the afternoon because they won't be there. But given that there are periods of the day when such fights are possible, what, we must ask, are the rules which will govern the instigation of fights. On what basis do fans attack or refrain from attacking rivals given that the opportunity for attacks exists?

On the basis of a careful observation it is possible to describe conflicts and fights at a very basic level. One can record, for example whose fist or boot made contact with whom and with which part of the body. But this does not allow us to say what a fight is. Does the sequence of events which have been described as taking place at half-time constitute a fight even though no blows have been exchanged or would fans give some other interpretation? We might think that we have a very good idea of what a fight is, but there is no way of knowing, at this stage, whether our conceptions of fights are in accord with those of football fans. If we were to press on regardless and attempt to explain the basis for fights among fans in our own terms we would be unlikely to produce an explanation which had relevance to anything other than the kinds of interpretation we brought to the analysis in the first place. It is, therefore, with the commonsense construal by fans of fights and other conflict encounters that the second stage of a discovery procedure must be concerned.

Our interest in seeing how fans construe fights is not simply a function of perverse whim but rather can be seen as deriving indirectly from the work of people such as Robin Fox. In his account of fights among rural Irishmen on Tory Island, Fox (1977) reveals a distinctly rule-governed type of conflict resolution. Here everyone talks of the 'grand fights' for days after the event and yet in the fights themselves the protagonists very rarely come to blows at all. They shout imprecations at each other and they make fist-swinging gestures but these fists usually fail to get anywhere near the opponent's body. Fox also points out the roles adopted by onlookers and the rather comic situations produced by their intervention:

> There was a lull in the movement during which both principals came forward yelling at each other. The insults rose in pitch and complexity until Johnny, provoked beyond words, tore off his coat and threw it on the ground.
>
> Now this is a serious matter on Tory. 'I'll take off me coat' – this is an invitation to a real fight. As long as the coat stays on, serious fighting is not intended. . . .
>
> The coat was immediately retrieved by his group and desperate attempts were made to get it back on him again. At this point, a newcomer could be forgiven for thinking that the fight was between Johnny and those who had his coat, for he was inflicting more damage on them than he would ever get to inflict on Paddy.

What Fox describes is essentially a system of rules which have the effect of turning conflicts between two men into large-scale social events. The intervention of supporters of each of the fighters occurs in a regular and orderly way and has the effect of both prolonging the fight and of making sure that neither of the protagonists injure each other. There is a kind of social contract between each fighter and his friends and relations in the onlooking crowd. 'Hold me back or I'll kill him,' says the fighter and the crowd does just this. The result – nobody is killed.

The parallels between what happens on Tory Island and events at football matches are very striking indeed. From the standpoint of an observer it seemed that soccer fans were similarly entering into situations which would be called 'fights' but which also were the subject of social controls and restraints. The task, therefore, became that of revealing the rules upon which such controls and restraints were founded.

Earlier we pointed to the problems which arise when one asks questions without having the appropriate knowledge or conceptual tools to deal with the answers. But questions such as 'What should one do in a fight?' or 'What do you do when you put the boot in?' must be asked at some stage, and a rule-discovery procedure must be capable of rendering answers to such questions intelligible. In working towards this, we believe, attention must be given to the *active* process by which fans negotiate meanings among themselves. For most of the time concepts of fights and conflicts are taken for granted within the soccer culture. They form a set of background meanings which are tacitly assumed but there is rarely occasion to question them. If, however, we make the taken-for-granted aspects of everyday social life on the terraces problematic to fans, we can begin to reveal more precisely the constituents and structure of this semantic 'backdrop'. If we were to follow Garfinkel we might actually get among the action and upset its steady flow. We might interfere and disrupt routine social events in order to show up what the tacit assumptions are. To do this on the terraces, however, would require a very brave and slightly suicidal social investigator. If it is the case, as will be argued in more detail later, that the terrace rules serve to prevent the potentially bloody outcomes of a state of aggression, then disruption of routine social events based on such rules might indeed prove to have serious consequences.

The taken-for-granted aspects of the fans' social world can, of course, be made problematic in a much less dramatic way. The strategy employed in our study has been to make fans' *accounts* problematic and to present them with descriptions and video-recordings of naturally occurring events which are *a priori* problematic. In essence, this involves the use of relatively simple techniques – methods which stand in contradiction to the notion that rendering actors' accounts intelligible involves an almost mystical process.

In dealing with accounts the task is to reveal how situations, events and actions are rendered meaningful within the terms of reference of the person giving the account. In doing this, however, one is not trying to see how what a fan says *fits* with what might be seen as the objective facts of the situation he describes. Rather, objective data allows for a contrast to be made when examining the terms of reference being used. In listening to accounts we are not involved in trying to hear the *truth* because, as we have insisted, an 'event' may have any number of 'truths'. Similarly we cannot assume that when an account appears to us to contain incon-sistencies it will also appear as being inconsistent to other fans. The small piece of transcript given earlier seems a clear case of incon-sistent accounting. The following one reveals these apparent inconsistencies in more detail and is very typical of the kind of material which fans provide. It also shows, however, how it might be possible to explain the fact that accounts given by fans appear to represent conflicts as being bloody and dangerous and at the same time as involving relatively little injury.

Interviewer: I'd just like you to talk about some of the things that happen at football matches – things you've actually seen or been involved in. Later on I'll play back the tape and ask you a few questions.

Paul: Well last week up against Sunderland at the Manor there was a lot of trouble. Same as last year. They come down and we've got something to – well we've got a kind of needle because of what they did last year. There's bound to be a lot of trouble really.

Wayne: Those Sunderland fans think they're really hard – they always go looking for trouble so they get it, don't they? There was bottles flying there all over the place and this Sunderland kid had some of those Kung Fu stars – he was chucking them at us – you've got to do something, so me and a pile of other kids went round the back and up into their bit of the terrace and that's when all the trouble started. The police couldn't do very much – we were all in there too quick. They just had to stand and watch.

Paul: We don't go looking for trouble – not now – but if it comes at you you've got no choice.

Patrick: The coppers couldn't care really so long as they don't get hurt. You can have some kids really kicking you and they don't do nothing 'cos they're scared of getting it themselves. At the Sunderland match there was one old boy on the floor with a pile of kids with their red scarves going over him – and there's another small kid with blood all on his face and shirt, and the coppers are just looking. They don't try to stop it.

Dennis: They got old Steve though. He's got to go to court in about a month's time just 'cos he tried to get rid of some Sunderland out of the London Road. These kids come in round the side and Steve and some of the big Townies grabbed hold of two of them and gave them a kicking. These three coppers come in and they're not doing nothing about the Sunderland kids – they just pick on Steve and take him out to the van.

Paul: It really gets bad at times like that – bottles and bricks flying through the air. Some of the kids have got knives and steel combs – one kid I saw had this bit of copper pipe with the end all filed down to make it sharp – it could make a hole right through you.

Wayne: Kids go charging in – there's boots flying all over – real mad sometimes. With teams like Sunderland – they're mad – just lash out. So now we try to get the boot in first – as they arrive and before they can get together. You can get the boot in first and maybe scare them off a bit. We got a couple as they were coming up from their coach and they didn't know what hit them. It makes them think, don't it?

[*After about ten minutes the tape was stopped and the four fans listened to what they had said. The interviewer had said nothing up to this point.*]

Interviewer: Let's look at some of the things you've been saying and try to fill in some of the details. First of all, what kind of picture do you get when you listen to that?

Paul: Well, it sounds a bit bad, doesn't it? It's not really always like – not always as bad as that. It's atmosphere really – it's sort of electric – it gets you going. Even when you're telling about it – when you look back over it and think about it – you can feel the atmosphere.

Patrick: When you're in there with all your mates – well, you can't put it into words.

Interviewer: The match against Sunderland seems to stand out, judging by what you've said, as being more – well as having more trouble than the others this season. How many people do you think got hurt last week – by hurt I mean actually bleeding or getting a bone broken or having to get some treatment or something like that.

Paul: Not many really. You get kids with bloody noses. . . .

Wayne: Do you mean getting all cut up and that? – hardly nobody – you don't see much of that. Sometimes you get it like that kid who got stabbed at Blackpool.

Paul: It's all exaggerated most of the time – when you read about it in the papers and they say that kids is getting almost killed and that. I mean – you wouldn't want to go in there.

Interviewer: Why is it that not too many people get hurt, do you think?

Paul: I don't know really. You just want to rough them up a bit I suppose.

Patrick: Except for me – I want to kill them.

Interviewer: When you go in against the opposition fans do you go in with the idea of just roughing them up or . . .

Paul: Oh no – when you're out to get them you don't care how you do it. But when you've got them or they're maybe running back – well then you've got better things to do.

Wayne: That's right – somebody always runs. . . .

Patrick: Usually Oxford.

Wayne: One lot always runs when they see they're going to get a hammering. So that way it's only a few nutters who hang around who are asking to get smashed up.

Paul: Sometimes things get bad – like when I saw some kids get trampled on last season at Man. United. They'd got on the floor and everybody was just jumping on them as they were trying to get out of it. But it's usually just a few kids who get roughed up or smacked in the mouth.

Wayne: You goes in there – sort of going in to nut people, or give them a kicking or something like that. But, normally, anyway, the kids don't get all beaten up. You can tell when somebody's had enough – really you're trying to stop them giving you a lot of mouth. You get mad at them but you know when to stop.

From this piece of transcript it is quite clear that fans are capable of giving two very different accounts concerning what happens in conflict situations. At one level, and particularly in the first part of the transcript, they present a picture of violence and destruction – fans get 'booted', 'nutted' and generally beaten up and bottles and flying bricks result in bloodied victims. At a second level, a picture of orderly conflict is presented in which fans make a lot of noise, put on a big show but are really trying to stop the opposition from 'giving a lot of mouth' rather than seriously trying to injure them.

The temptation when faced with this kind of material is to try to read consistency into it by 'leaning' on it somewhat. One might argue, quite reasonably, that when a fan says that someone got 'smashed up' he means something other than the fan was hurt – that he is using the term in a manner which follows different rules of interpretation from those which apply outside of the soccer culture. One might appeal to the special nature of the semantic rules existing on the terraces which give rise only to the appearance of inconsistency in fans' accounts. Such approaches, however, would be totally inappropriate in this case. However much we analyse accounts, and however much we examine in detail the conceptual systems which generate accounts, the inconsistencies remain. Put simply, the inconsistencies derive from the fact that football fans construct not a single reality but two distinct realities. On the one hand they view events on the terraces as being bloody and dangerous, and on the other they see the same events as orderly and safe. The plurality of fans' accounts cannot be explained away by an appeal to the special nature of everyday language use among soccer supporters. Although this may seem to pose a problem in the explanation of fans' social behaviour, such a disjointed view is to be expected for a number of very good reasons.

First, given the inevitability of a number of viewpoints existing in respect of something that as far as place and time are concerned is a single phenomenon, it would be unreasonable to expect such view-points to be independent of each other. Rather, we should expect a predictable type of interaction among them. In the introduction reference was made to the outside model as encapsulating the 'controllers' theory'. Such a theory generates a reality for those in positions of power and authority in society which might be inter-preted as the 'hegemonic' ideology. It is this ideology which is given currency in the newspapers, on television and in discussions among the right-thinking, often outraged, decent majority. We also have very strong evidence concerning the degree to which this ideology can influence the inside model constructed by those who are involved in the social events themselves and who become labelled as deviant. Changes in the attitudes and actions of the controllers lead to new reactions on the part of deviants who in turn are seen as provoking new official strategies and measures. But more impor-tantly, some aspects of the controllers' theory become 'internalized' by the deviant group. In other words, not only is there an easily explained reaction to official theories and attitudes, and the meas-ures taken on the basis of these, but also some very real acceptance on the part of the deviants of the hegemonic ideology.

There are, as will be made clear, some very good reasons why fans would wish to incorporate some aspects of the dominant view of 'hooliganism' into their own social reality. Such incorporation, it must be noted, is not to be mistaken for the rather superficial reflection of hegemonic ideology which social scientists are forever encountering in their work. When one uses a questionnaire, for example, the 'responses' are inevitably a reflection of what is per-ceived by 'subjects' to be the appropriate translation of the domin-ant and respectable view. Questionnaires elicit responses which are thought to be appropriate in answering questionnaires. The *Sun* newspaper once commissioned Marplan to conduct a questionnaire survey on soccer hooliganism. 'How serious is the problem of soccer hooliganism?' it asked. 'Very serious' replied 45 per cent of the sample. Everybody knows that soccer hooliganism is a serious problem because that is what newspapers like the *Sun* are always telling us, and that is the reply which will be seen as appropriate to a questionnaire. Now in using the more sensitive techniques involved in participation, observation and elicitation of members' accounts we can avoid some of these problems, but we cannot do so entirely. We must expect, at least initially, some aspects of the hegemonic ideology to appear in fans' accounts and talk because we, as social scientists, will inevitably be seen as belonging to the outside. *However*, we strongly assert that the reflection of the dominant view-point contained in one aspect of fans' talk is not simply an artefact of the research methodology. We see it as constituting one of two realities which fans are able to entertain simultaneously. In order to explain this apparently 'schizoid' view of their social world we appeal to a *conspiracy* on the part of football fans.

The theme of this book has been that apparently disordered events on the football terraces and in the classroom can be seen as conforming to a very distinct and orderly system of roles, rules and shared meanings. Action is neither chaotic nor senseless but rather is structured and reasoned. Later we will argue that in the case of football fans this order derives from the very basic need of any society to possess social mechanisms by which aggression among its members can be controlled and managed. At this point in the development of the theme, however, we need to consider some expected consequences of order. One such consequence, we believe, is a conspiracy on the part of members of an orderly sub-culture to deny that order exists.

In conspiring to construct a reality which seems to be at variance with their tacit knowledge of orderly and rule-governed action, fans are engaged in the active creation (and adoption from the outside) of excitement. For fans, regularity and safety are things to be avoided. They are quite simply 'a drag'. What the soccer terraces offer is a chance to escape from the dreariness of the weekday world of work or school to something which is adventurous and stimulating. But in order to achieve the contrast it is necessary to construe, at least at one level, the soccer terraces as being radically different from the weekday world. School and work are safe and regular. *Ergo*, soccer terraces are potentially dangerous and unpredictable. Since fans 'know' that this is not the case – they are aware and can tell you that few people get hurt even when things 'get out of hand' – they must conspire to construct disorder. And because there is an easy rhetoric to hand – the rhetoric of the media which insists that events at football matches are *in fact* disordered, the conspiracy is an easy one to conduct.

Not only is such a conspiracy instrumental in achieving excitement and anticipation, it is also essential in the establishment and maintenance of careers. Certain roles would clearly not be available to fans unless conflict situations were capable of being perceived as requiring acts of courage and determination. If fights were seen as being purely ceremonial affairs involving no risk of injury, then the status of a fighter would be of very little value at all. But the status of aggro leader, as we have seen, affords the occupant a good deal of deference and kudos. There is a strong belief that such a person is ready to deal with any of the consequences that arise in challenging rival groups of fans. The emptiness of this belief is only removed if there exists a reality in which conflicts do indeed regularly lead to bloody end-products.

The idea of a conspiracy of this kind, then, is theoretically very plausible. Not only is it to be expected, it can be seen as a necessary consequence of an orderly system such as the one with which we are concerned. But besides being theoretically possible, the conspiracy process can actually be observed. Many examples are evident from conversations between fans in a variety of settings. The one we offer here is taken from talk between four fans on a special coach. The conversation is reconstructed from notes made at the time and although it is not reported verbatim it is a good representation of what was said.

A note concerning the background to the story is required. A coach had been hired by fans, under the management of one of the organizers, to take them to a match against Southampton. On arriving fans found to their dismay that the game had been cancelled because the ground was waterlogged. (The organizer was the subject of some censure for not having checked on this before setting out.) The Oxford fans, faced with the prospect of a wasted Saturday, persuaded the coach driver to take them to Swindon, who happened to be at home to Walsall. Swindon are Oxford's arch rivals from the days when they used to play in the same division and the prospect of having a rare opportunity to 'have a go' at them almost compensated for not being able to see Oxford play. The coach arrived at Swindon just after the kick-off and about fifty Oxford fans entered the ground chanting insults and imprecations at the Swindon 'wankers' and threatening to take their End. Walsall supporters were much bemused at having such uninvited allies but having as little love for them as they had for the Swindon fans, refused to join them in their assault on Swindon's End. Even on a bad day in the Third Division, an End can hold several hundred Rowdies and the odds against the fifty Oxford fans making more than a mere token gesture of occupying the End were rather high. There was a brief pushing scuffle as about twenty of the fitter Oxford boys tried to squeeze their way into the crowd, but they were pushed out again and sent back to the other end of the pitch. The rest of the match passed without incident and some fans even went back to the coach early because it was raining quite hard. Out of such an uninspiring day, however, fans were able to construct a very much more exciting reality.

Keith: Did you see that big fat cunt of a copper when we was in the Swindon End? There's this Swindon boy with a beer can and he chucks it at us – but when we tries to get him the copper grabs me by the hair and slings me out.

Danny: Yeah – if it weren't for the coppers we could have walked in there – right over them.

Keith: Cunts.

Dave: That kid on the floor though – old John gave him a real good kicking – lost some teeth I reckon.

Ross: Was that the kid with blood on his face – sort of ginger hair – stupid looking?

Dave: No – he had black hair – had black hair, didn't he Keith?

Keith: I dunno – I didn't see it.

Dave: You must have done. We were right together. The kid on the floor getting kicked.

Keith: Oh him. But what about when we first run in and this old boy makes a grab at – at Terry wasn't it? Hey Terry – what happened to that old boy who made a grab at you?

[*Terry doesn't hear because he's sitting much further back in the coach*]

Keith: Deaf cunt. No, but I saw this old boy and he's sort of holding his head like he got nutted or something.

[*John, sitting in the seat behind Keith and Dave has been quietly listening*]

John: You bullshitter, Matthews.

Keith: No, straight John – he got hit on the head or something. Terry really got him I reckon.

Dave: Swindon are bloody easy – if they were to come up to the Manor still we'd kick shit out of them.

Danny: Just one bus load of us and we walked straight in there. If it weren't for the coppers we could have just stayed there.

A song starts up . . .

> We took Swindon and all them in it,
> We took Swindon in half a minute.
> With hatchets and hammers,
> Carving knives and spanners . . .

The example is no more than a slightly comic vignette and yet it shows up quite clearly the way in which conspiracies are managed. Fans 'knew' that very little had happened and in fact said so when asked to talk about the match during the following week. But by the time the coach had arrived back in Oxford on the Saturday evening the day had been made remarkable and worthy of being talked about. (See also the analysis made by Paul Corrigan, forthcoming.)

Many other examples could be offered on the basis of listening to the social talk of football fans – some aspects of the conspiracy being made even more visible by incorporation into the repertoire of chants. '*We're gonna do to you what we did to Villa*' is one which crops up from time to time and is thought to be very menacing. Fans know, and will tell you, that what they did to Aston Villa supporters was simply to push them all out of the stand and on to the pitch where they milled around looking very humiliated. But they also know that it is preferable to believe that Villa fans were massacred in a bloody onslaught against them.

In making this detour into a consideration of conspiracy, and the consequent dual system of realities which fans entertain, a basic requirement for the understanding of fans' accounts emerges. Unless the point is taken seriously, what fans say is at best enigmatic and at worst totally unintelligible. In trying to uncover a rule structure we are faced not with the task of discriminating between fantasy and reality but between one reality and another. It just so happens that this task turns out to be a little easier in practice than it might sound. As will be illustrated, the accounts which fans give, by and large, are such that identification of the two frames of reference is not too problematic. It might also be useful to stress at this point that fans have not in any way been pressurized into giving statements which fit with our expectations of order. On the contrary, fans were asked to participate by simply talking about what happens on the terraces, answering some probing but non-directing questions and in some cases to comment on their own accounts. The suspicion that the view of danger and violence which fans offer is the only 'real' one, and that the second view of order is simply a product of the way questions have been put, is without foundation. The view of order and rules often emerges without the necessity of asking any questions at all and it should be clear from the transcripts we offer below that questions are asked only in order to seek clarification or detail.

The following pieces of transcript are taken from a series of about fifty interviews. Each interview session lasted, on average, about an hour and involved between two to four fans at a time. The examples given are not specially selected ones – much of what is contained in them is very typical and representative of what the other fans had to say. We present them as data for the isolation of rules.

Interviewer: So, what is necessary before fights actually take place or before any trouble starts? Why weren't there any fights at Notts County last week, for example?

Mark: All the trouble-makers support Forest mostly [the other major football team in Nottingham] – that's why there was no trouble at County.

Mike: The year before when we went up to Notts County, we got off the coach and I asked this policeman where the away supporters stand and he goes 'Oh anywhere. All the trouble makers are at Forest.' So . . . and County never had many supporters really. What it seemed – they were smaller – not that many big people there – but Oxford didn't really have enough to go round there [to County's End] – there wasn't enough really. Neither side wanted to start anything. Oxford might have done if we'd been really beaten – but it's difficult to say.

Interviewer: Why are there people fighting in the first place at some games. What's your explanation?

Mike: Well – I suppose if there's enough of you the idea is sort of to take the other team's End.

Interviewer: For what reason?

Mike: Well it's something to boast about.

Interviewer: Do you think that's all it's about – so that some people can establish a reputation, or is there more to it?

Mike: No, I wouldn't say that that's all it's for. It plays a part – a large part I think. You get people who are naturally aggressive – that get mad at the first sign of anything – that are always looking for trouble wherever it is.

Mark: Manchester United people are like that.

Mike: Well – I don't know – some small ones are just as mad.

Interviewer: Let's try to examine just what happens when fights do occur – stage by stage through a typical example – either between two large groups of people or between individuals . . .

Mike: On the terraces?

Interviewer: Yes, on the terraces or outside of the ground – What actually goes on?

Mark: Well, at Oxford it's mainly when someone tries to come round the Oxford supporters' side.

Mike: You've got your two gangs of people on the terraces and elsewhere, and while they're a distance away from each other they'll all go in together but as soon as they're fairly close to each other – it's the people at the back who push and those at the front don't have much choice really, they get flung into it.

Interviewer: Take the case when a few people have come round into the London Road End. They appear in your part of the terrace. What do you do as a result of that?

Mike: Well, us Oxford kids just go mad at that – if there's enough or if there's big enough people. They'll go through the smaller people like a knife through butter, sort of thing.

Interviewer: Doing what?

Mike: Well just push away and then they shout about or if they've got scarves on – then the bigger kids, well anyone really, they'll just have a go.

Interviewer: In 'having a go' what do you do?

Mike:　Just lash out . . .

Mark:　Boot them . . .

Mike:　Hit them, nut them – anything – depends on how close you are.

Interviewer:　In terms of inflicting damage on someone – to what extent does that occur?

Mike:　Well – even when you go into something like that and someone gets kicked about a bit – there's not usually much damage that gets done. The Millwall supporters that come in – I don't think many were seriously hurt, couple of cuts perhaps – And Villa supporters – just bruises I think – nothing bad. When Sunderland come in – that was a bit worse because it was before the match and there wasn't so much of a crowd – and one of them got kicked to the ground.

Mark:　When was that?

Mike:　Not last season but the season before that. Some Sunderland supporters came in before the start of the match – about three-quarters of an hour before. And Oxford just come at them – they got kicked to the ground.

Mark:　Was that when Hugh Curran was up the London Road End?

Mike:　No, that's three years ago – well it was a bit more serious then.

Interviewer:　You seem to be saying that people don't get hurt all that often – rather bruised or something like that – not seriously . . .

Mike:　That's right.

Interviewer:　Do you think that when people are going into fights or 'getting mad' that they aren't deliberately trying to hurt other people very much?

Mike:　Oh yes.

Interviewer:　Do you mean they are actually setting out to hurt them?

Mike:　Yes – well you're just swinging around and when it's packed out and everybody's pushing to get at the same people – you can't really take any swings at anybody – it's, well, just feeble efforts really.

Interviewer:　Take fights between two people – one from either side, when there *is* room to actually hurt someone. To what extent do people get hurt in those sort of fights?

Mark:　It's more like a wrestling match really.

Mike:　That's right – you don't get anything that serious.

Interviewer:　It would seem to me to be quite possible for two people in those situations to bash hell out of each other . . .

Mike: Yes, it would seem like that but it seldom tends to happen that way.

Interviewer: What exactly *does* happen? How do fights between two people actually start? Take an example which seems to happen a lot. You're outside the ground and there's a group of you and a group of them. And there's one leading figure in each group. These two leading figures shout insults at each other. That seems to be a very commonplace thing.

Mark: Yes.

Mike: Sure.

Interviewer: Sometimes it turns into a fight and sometimes it doesn't.

Mike: More often it doesn't because one usually breaks away. It's usually long-range stuff – shouting – and if one shows he's not scared of the other and goes towards the other – the other usually ends up running away in both cases.

Interviewer: Say you've got two equally strong personalities – what happens if neither breaks down?

Mark: They come straight into each other.

Mike: Yes.

Mark: And then one starts to get the worst of it and they all kind of run.

Mike: I haven't known that much – except for one incident and that was against Sheffield Wednesday two years ago. I went up with a friend of mine – he's a year older than me – about 18 – he's really sort of tough and he's a black belt at judo although he'd never use it at football – really hard. There was all these Sheffield everywhere. We were wearing scarves. There was me, him and another chap the same age as me. We got off the bus and there was this big bloke – looked as if he'd been in the forces – short-back-and-sides hair cut. We walked by them and they both made a comment at each other. And my mate, he turned round and shouted something back at this Sheffield Wednesday supporter. And they both went at each other. The Sheffield supporter took a swing at my mate and he ducked out of the way of it. Then my mate took a swing back and just caught him but he slipped up so the Sheffield supporter just jumped on top. It was just sort of like the Sheffield supporter trying to hold him down. Well we broke it up in the end. It only happened a couple of minutes.

Interviewer: What do you think would happen if you turned up to a football match and there were absolutely no policemen there?

Tiz: One side would run.

George: And fast.

Tiz: I reckon that one side would clear off completely.

Interviewer: What, before any fighting had started at all?

Tiz: No, they might square up to them for a little while – but if they started to get the worst of it they'd soon run.

George: There would always be the odd occasion . . .

Tiz: Yes, there would always be one or two who'd stay until put in hospital or something like that – but the majority would disappear.

Interviewer: Do you think people would be so brave if there were no police?

Tiz: No way.

Interviewer: Do you think people rely on the police to stop fights?

Tiz: That's right – they're mainly shouting about trying to show that they're hard but with the knowledge that the police are there if anything gets out of hand or if they can't get away.

Interviewer: I was talking to some of your mates yesterday and they were saying that most fights – that in most fights not many people get hurt and that when there are fights there's usually some reason for it. They also said that you two were thought of as being quite hard . . .

Tiz: Who said that?

George: I'll kick his head in.

Tiz: No seriously – it's true few people get really hurt. It's the same when I used to live in London a couple of years ago. You get lots of scraps – well that's natural like – but it's only one or two who get really done over.

Interviewer: What about the reasons for fighting?

Tiz: Well, of course there's reasons for fighting. I mean, if somebody walks up and calls you a cunt you're going to have to do something about it. Sometimes you might be – well you might see one or two fans of another team and – well you take a disliking to them so you might want to go over and give them a bit of needle – take the piss a bit. And then maybe one of them will take a dislike to you and have a go at you so you've got to do something about that.

George: Most matches you get this. You get someone screwing you [staring] or just standing there all cocky like so someone's got to go and take him down a peg or two.

George: When you get some of the other side's fans in your End – that's when the trouble really starts. It's your territory – your property – it's like someone just walking into your house or something like that. Well you just have to get them out one way or another. You can't stand for that. . . . But you see a lot of people imagine that you're some kind of wild animal – just going crazy and diving into people. Well there are some kids like that . . .

Tiz: Like Phil English . . .

George: Yes he's one – but the rest of us, well we're not so stupid. You've got to think a bit. You're not going to let – I mean you're not going to stand for kids just fucking you about. But you're not going to stand around and get beaten into the ground when there's too many of them. The other week we were on Magdalen Bridge – just minding our own business – and this pile of Bristol City fans come pelting over towards us. Well we just upped and ran off – no use in being done over to prove a point. They only chased for a bit though and then carried on down to the station.

Interviewer: Do you think that people know when to stop in fights?

Tiz: Most people. You get some people who go too far or just get carried away – but you can usually tell when someone's had enough.

George: When they stop giving you any lip or run then you've done what you wanted to do. If you carry on – well, the police will soon get on the scene for one thing. Like – well, if we see an Oxford fan and he's having some barny with one of the visiting fans – well you leave him to get on with it. But if a crowd of them come over and start hammering into him well then you have to go and help him out. Same really if there's one of their lot who's had enough but someone's carrying on too far with him. Well, we'll go over and pull him off.

Tiz: Sometimes people do get really smashed up. There was one geezer down at Chelsea who got his skull fractured and some broken ribs. It was against Manchester United and these United fans – in fact they were London kids but Man. U. supporters – they'd streamed out after the match and out round to the back and he somehow got split off from the rest and got in the way of all these charging alone. I don't think anyone knew what was going on then – they sort of just slammed into him and that was that. But that doesn't happen much – you read about that sort of thing in the papers.

These two examples are probably sufficient to show that fans perceive fights as having a particular kind of structure to them. It is quite clear, for instance, that they have a knowledge of certain rules for the instigation of fights. On the terraces, territorial invasion constitutes a legitimation of attack. In small-group encounters, either on the concourse of the football club or outside of the ground, there is a distinct framework for the issuing and acceptance of challenges. Staring, or 'screwing', is seen as an invitation to fight even though the stare might not be deliberately intended. A more formal challenge is achieved simply by calling someone a cunt. In this case the person to whom the remark is directed must respond or risk the possibility of losing face.

In addition to rules which govern the specific form that challenges may take, there are certain rules which legitimate the issue of a challenge in the first place. One must have, it seems, a reason for making a challenge. The most basic requirement is that a rival must have some tokens of allegiance to the opposition team. Usually the fact that the fan is wearing a scarf of the 'wrong' colour will be a necessary condition, but not a sufficient one, for attacking him.*

Fans who are not wearing scarves or who have taken them off will rarely be challenged even though they might still be recognized as rivals and supporters of the other team. In fact, fans quite regularly refer to the process of concealing one's scarf as a tactical defensive manoeuvre.

As well as the stare, certain postures can be adopted in making threats or can be taken to constitute a threat by rivals. References to such postures crop up regularly in accounts in forms such as 'he was standing sort of cocky'. From our observations, such postures often take the form of an apparently dominant stance with one hand on the hips. Leaning against a wall and standing on one leg with the opposite foot bracing the body against the wall, would also, in all probability, be perceived as threatening.

Events external to the groups of fans are often seen as warranting attacks. There is frequent reference in the justificatory accounts of fans to the fact that the other team had scored a goal. It is at times like this that the chant *'You're gonna get your fucking head kicked in'* is most frequently heard. The fact that the other team might win the match as a result of the goal they have scored is frequently used as a justification for having a go at their supporters.

Certain types of foul play on the pitch are also seen as warranting some hostile action towards the opposition fans. It is not so much the foul play itself which gives this legitimation but rather the failure of the referee adequately to impose sanctions on the offending player. At times like this it appears that the fans take it upon themselves to enforce sanctions by punishing, or appearing ready to punish, the supporters of the offender.

Initiating attacks in the pursuit of territorial gain requires no further justification. An End is fair game at anytime – it is there to

---

* There is, however, a standard ritual on the terraces which involves the taking of rivals' scarves. One might find several home fans wearing the scarves of the visiting team, but these are trophies. It is not surprising, therefore, that the wearing of an 'alien' scarf can never, in itself, justify attacking its wearer. It could well be one's own fellow supporter showing off his spoils of war.

be taken by force because its very presence constitutes a threat to the rival fans. As we mentioned earlier, territories are action-facilitating – they are seen by fans as in themselves, warranting certain strategies and moves directed at occupying them. Similarly, references to territorial violation occur frequently in accounts of fights. The presence of someone from the opposing side in one's own well-delineated territory constitutes a good and just reason for 'nutting', 'booting' and 'lashing out' at him. Such is the inevitability of being attacked in the opposition's End that special possibilities for 'hazarding' and character demonstrations are provided as a result. One such form of hazarding consists of edging one's way through the entire opposition territory without being detected and without being violently thrown out. This feat is known to some fans as a 'walk through' and those who manage to carry off the enterprise gain a good deal of credit among their peers.

The basic point which emerges from this is, of course, that fights, at both the large group and the face-to-face level, do not start up randomly. They occur in circumstances which fans are able to specify and which are seen as legitimizing their actions.

The consistency with which fans are able to perceive the symbolic nature of fighting is most interesting. They all, with only one or two exceptions, maintain that few people get hurt, but they go further to indicate what they see as the major purposes of fighting. We note frequent reference to notions such as 'having something to boast about', 'being big' and so on. Not only do they apply these interpretations to the actions of others (which we might expect to some degree) but they also refer to themselves in this way.

The symbolic, as opposed to intentionally injurious, nature of fights is revealed in fans' conceptions of their orderliness and pre-dictability. There is a general consensus that there are limits beyond which one should not go. These limits are detectable in fans' refer-ences to breaches of constraints – for example, when people 'go mad' or 'have a fit'. The nutter who breaks the rules in this way needs restraining by the rest of the group around him at the time and at a particular point in the conflict encounter. By identifying the moment when intervention is seen as being required a knowledge of the legitimate boundaries of fights can be obtained.

In general there is agreement concerning when an opponent has had enough, and this occurs quite often after very little has appar-ently happened. It would seem, on the basis of what fans say, that only one or two blows at the most are required to settle even the most venomous face-to-face conflict. 'A smack in the mouth is all that is needed.' Those fans who go much further than this and continue the fight beyond the point where honour is seen to be satisfied do so at the risk of censure. Equally, however, certain submissive or appeasement signals are required from the loser. As Mike and Mark pointed out, there will always be the odd few who stand their ground until 'put in hospital', but in the main a fan perceiving that he is faced with a more determined and stronger opponent, or that his group is seriously outnumbered, will back down. In backing down, the loser has to do very little more than cease any actions which might be construed as hostile or threatening – he has to keep quiet or 'button his lip'. He should also look down at the floor – never at his opponent. Once he has done this he is unlikely to be attacked further even though he may have received only mild and relatively non-injurious blows during the encounter. This rapid closing off of fight sequences has more than a passing resemblance to the 'cut off' in the agonistic behaviour of animals, and more will be said about this in the next chapter.

The other way of closing off fights is, of course, for the loser to flee from the danger area, and this happens very regularly. To do so does not, in itself, mean that the person who runs will lose face. A fan who is outnumbered can run away from the scene even before there has been opportunity for any fighting at all and still not lose any credit among his peers. As Tiz and George pointed out, it would be sheer folly to hang around to get your 'head kicked in' if it could be avoided. To run is a legitimate and tactical piece of self-preservation in many circumstances. The fact that it happens with great regularity is reflected in the following song:

We had joy, we had fun,
We had Fulham on the run,
But the joy didn't last
Cos the bastards ran too fast.

Having people on the run, it would seem, is the name of the game – it is the major intention in fights and it produces victories which are highly visible. The opposition fans may run as a tactical retreat, and therefore not feel badly about it, but the fans who are doing the chasing can feel elated at their achievements. The chasing, it should also be noted, does not last for very long and there is usually a visible reluctance on the part of the pursuers ever to catch up with the group they are chasing. If this were to happen then fans suggest, a rather difficult situation would be produced and people might actually get hurt. Fans would not know what to do in such cases. Retreat and deference moves would have been exhausted and there would be no easily recognized system for deciding a 'winner'. It is therefore, very fortunate that the situation arises only very rarely.

One very interesting feature which is revealed both in the accounts that fans offer and in the careful observation of what they do is that of *fear*. It is this manifest fear that fans experience in conflict situations which, we feel, is very much reflected in the plurality of the accounts. Many fans, for example, talk of 'shitting themselves' when faced with menacing groups of rivals even though they also are clearly aware that few people (unless they are very foolish) actually come to grief in those circumstances. The fear is experienced at a very basic and physiological level – we have seen many fans exhibiting the classic fear symptoms of turning pale, sweating, hair erection and so on when coping with serious conflict encounters. It may well be that the conspiracy to perceive events as dangerous and disordered is both a product and a precipitator of this biologically based response.

The fear displayed here is almost analogous to something like vertigo. To experience fear one does not necessarily have to believe, at a rational level, that one is likely to come to any serious harm. Many people when standing on the top of a tall building feel insecure and afraid despite the fact that they know there is little danger of them falling off and being injured. Even mountaineers have this kind of experience. No matter how well developed one's rock-climbing skills are, and no matter how well protected one is with ropes and slings, one can still feel afraid when delicately stepping out on to a crag with only several hundred feet of fresh air beneath it. But perhaps this gives us some clues to the motivations of football fans. The rock climber gains his satisfaction from over-coming his natural fear responses and skilfully working his way to the top of a rock face. It is equally possible that the football fan gains in a similar way by overcoming his fear in hostile social encounters. By being a member of a group which places great emphasis on coping in this way, and which affords great esteem to those who do so courageously, the fan gains doubly.

All this is to throw some light on the fact that fans see fights as being orderly and rule governed and yet, at the same time, can feel afraid in fights. More importantly, they can admit such fear and offer it as a rationalization and justification of their actions in certain circumstances.

At this point we can start to summarize the major elements of the rule structure as revealed in the explanations that fans offer concerning fights.

1   There is a set of interpretative rules which dictate when attacks on rival fans are appropriate. At the level of large-group con-frontations events such as territorial violation or unsanctioned fouls on the pitch are interpreted as warranting such attacks. At the level of face-to-face conflicts a distinct set of criteria is available for establishing the existence of threats or challenges. On top of this there is a well-defined set of *objectives* which in turn prescribe certain strategies in the pursuit of these objectives.

2   Once fights have legitimately been initiated, certain rules apply

concerning the course the fight should take. These rules reflect the perceived goals of fighting in the first place and it is clear that these objectives are much wider than the straightforward infliction of pain and physical hurt.

3   Rules have been isolated which govern the closing off and termination of fights. At the face-to-face level certain displays of deference and submission are recognized and the offering of these is usually sufficient to prevent further hostilities. At the large-group level, retreat is recognized as constituting sufficient reason for not pursuing the fight any further since forcing a retreat is one of the major objectives of the fight.

Within this structure, of course, more detailed rules exist and greater complexities can be introduced. Certain historical antecedents can also affect the applicability of even the most basic conventions. Fans from Swindon or Reading, for example, are considered to be targets for attack at any time simply by virtue of the fact that they support teams geographically close to Oxford. There is a long-standing antagonism towards them and one is not required to observe the niceties of conventionalized challenges. Similarly, one might be excused for inflicting more than the normal amount of physical hurt on them. Rarely, however, are the rules waived to such an extent that serious injuries result.

The rules isolated so far emerge quite clearly from the accounts that fans give concerning the reasons for their actions and in the ways that certain actions are seen as justifiable. As we pointed out at the beginning of this chapter, however, it would be unreasonable to expect fans to be consciously aware of the full range of conventions which govern their conduct at football matches. Although, on the basis of lengthy involvement and discussion with fans, we are able to isolate many of the most salient features of the rule framework, some of the more subtle aspects can only be discovered through techniques which focus on specific aspects of social action. One such method involves attention to the structure of certain episodes and action sequences which often do not figure prominently in fans' accounts. Consider the observed sequence outlined earlier in the discussion of events which take place at half-time near the tea stall at Oxford United's ground. Here we have a situation in which a Sheffield Wednesday fan is being taunted by an Oxford Rowdy. A stand-up conflict develops which is finally resolved by the intervention of one of the Town Boys. Many other examples like this exist but, assuming such episodes to be rule-governed, the problem remains of isolating just what the rules are. If the story is presented to fans they see it as being unremarkable – it is a commonplace event which they recognize but about which they generally have little to say. If, however, the story is presented with some aspects changed, or the sequential order altered, we find that the fans think that there is something wrong. By looking at what they say is wrong with the story we can obtain recognition of rule-breaches. This in turn allows us to specify what the rules themselves are. As an example, the story was presented as it was observed but the outcome was changed to:

> 'the Sheffield Wednesday fan called over some of his mates who grabbed hold of the Oxford boy who had been making the insults and took him away to give him a kicking.'

In a second example the outcome of the episode was changed to:

> 'the Sheffield Wednesday fan just got up and walked away.'

Stories such as these were presented to a number of fans and they were asked to comment on the 'correctness' or otherwise of the account. One fan, commenting on the first example had this to say:

> 'This kind of thing happens a lot. Kids start picking on one or two of the away lot – that's natural. But you don't get your mates into it like that – well only when there's too many of them or something and you're going to get kicked about or something like that. He could have just stood up or something and maybe they'd have had a bit of a go at each other. But nothing much would have come of it 'cos the Police are always around there and they'd soon move in. He's from Sheffield – I don't know – but he shouldn't get his mates in just for that – Oxford would get mad for that.'

Another fan commenting on the second example:

> 'You can't just walk off like that. He ought to have done something. An Oxford kid would have done something anyway I think. . . . He wasn't going to get smashed up or nothing – I mean, it's not like there was a big gang of them or anything – there's just this one kid and there's some other Sheffield there but they're not doing much. If I was in there I'd just – well I'd just turn round and maybe have a bit of a go or something. If it was some Sheffield kid coming on at me like that I'd just try and shut his mouth. You shouldn't walk off so that he can think he's big like.'

This simple technique yields a wealth of interesting information and can be applied to an analysis of the rules which operate in a wide range of situations. It is also possible to present records of naturally occurring events which seem, to the observer to have 'gone wrong'. Usually these consist of episodes which stand out as being 'non-typical' or 'irregular'. If events on the terraces were truly disordered then fans should see nothing surprising when presented with records of activities which resulted in physical injury or apparent chaos. The fact that they are able to point to specific factors which they see as precipitating a kind of 'breakdown' of the rule system is, perhaps, the most convincing demonstration of the falsehood of this notion. In anomic social situations, disorder requires no explanation – it is anticipated and has no 'reason' to it. Where social order exists, however, events which are disorderly require a good deal of explanation and where fans are able to point to good and sufficient reasons for the breakdown of order, we gain further evidence for the existence of a 'steady-state' system of rules and a sense of social propriety. Although we might disagree with what fans say in the sense that we do not see the reasons they propose in their explanations as being good or sufficient at all, we have to accept that, from the inside, there exists a framework in which certain actions can be justified or censured. The following example illustrates this point.

A number of Oxford fans were shown part of a video-recording which was made at Crystal Palace during their game with Plymouth Argyle. At half-time, two Argyle fans had run onto the pitch with a ball and started up their own game near the Palace End. Police rushed on to the field and started to chase the fans back towards the terrace where the Plymouth fans were standing. One policeman fell over, his helmet flying into a deep puddle of water. The two fans proved difficult to catch. More police were called out onto the pitch and finally one of the fans was brought down by a flying rugby tackle – to the cheers of Palace supporters. The other, however, managed to elude his pursuers and made it back into the Plymouth Argyle terrace before he could be arrested. A few minutes later, a group of about twenty policemen surged into the terrace from the rear in an attempt, one presumes, to retrieve the fan who had eluded capture. A large scuffle broke out and the police were forced to retreat. A fight started between a policeman and one of the Plymouth supporters at the back and several arrests were made. The police regrouped with reinforcements and charged back into the crowd. This time they managed to apprehend a number of fans and maintained their positions within the Plymouth crowd until the end of the match. Compared with some of the more spectacular events which occur from time to time at football games this incident was rather small and unimportant – it did not, for example, receive a mention in the national newspapers. But at the same time, the fans we talked to in Oxford consistently saw this event as something other than the normal activity one expects to see at football games and a number of features were isolated as being reasons for its occurrence.

First, they pointed out that there was nothing very unusual about fans running on to the pitch. 'They were only kicking a ball around – not doing much harm,' was a typical comment. They accepted, however, that the police had an obligation to remove them.

> 'Those coppers though, look there's about ten or fifteen of them and they're all running round in circles. And when they've got hold of one of them – there's three all pulling him about. One's got his arm round his neck and the others have got hold of his arms and they're really going into him.'

In general, there was a feeling that the police had totally mismanaged the whole affair. They had made unwarranted charges into the Argyle crowd and were seen as provoking fans beyond reasonable endurance. Now, presumably the police would have offered a totally different account of what went on and would have seen their measures as being justified by the fact that they had a responsibility for bringing offenders at football matches to justice. (We say 'presumably' because the police felt unwilling to make any comment and our video-camera crew were ordered to leave the ground immediately after the incident.)

The point which arises out of all this is that fans have a clear idea of how they think police and other officials at football games should act – in other words, they have rules for the actions of others as well as themselves and they are able to interpret some of the actions on the part of officials as being in breach of propriety. In the same way that kids in classrooms have a clear idea of what are the limits of legitimate action on the part of teachers, football fans appeal to the fact that the police 'went too far' or were 'making people a bit mad for no reason' in their explanation of certain events. One might argue that these imposed limits are unreasonable, but in the explanation of social action they figure very prominently and must therefore be given serious attention.

The fact that rules and order are to be found within the framework of social action on the terraces does not mean that all is sweetness and light at football matches. Indeed, it might be argued that the presence of a stable rule-system actually serves to perpetuate a range of activities which are thought to be anti-social or potentially harmful to society. To point to order among sub-cultures is not to excuse what members of sub-cultures do – the analysis of such order provides only for an explanation at one level and in one set of terms. In the next chapter, however, we turn to a consideration of what the real *function* of the rules on the football terraces might be. It is on the basis of this level of analysis that we feel the value of such order to society as a whole might be assessed.

5
Aggro as
Ritualized Aggression

Throughout the preceding discussion of order both in the classroom and on the football terraces there has been the theme of multiple realities. The notion that social events have an 'objective reality' independent of the active process whereby meanings are ascribed to them has been firmly resisted. Instead, we have pointed out that events such as those which occur at football matches are capable of being construed in a number of ways depending upon the viewpoint from which interpretations are made. From the inside the fans are able to provide accounts which illustrate the rule-directed aspects of activities at and around the soccer grounds. In contrast, those outside the football culture often believe, and at times forcibly maintain, that actions on the terraces are barbarically senseless and without reason. Similarly, we have seen that school kids have very different ways of construing apparently violent disturbances in the classroom from teachers involved in the same events. From a purely phenomenological point of view one might be tempted to leave it at that – to articulate the viewpoints and social realities which exist and invite readers to take their pick. And this would be a very reasonable stance to take since there is no adequate method for choosing between such social realities. One might wish to argue that some realities fit better with objective data than others but this is hardly the point. Realities are constructed in terms of subjective meanings and not in terms of objective facts. We can all recognize the facts that football trains are sometimes damaged and that both fans and policemen are sometimes injured. We might quarrel over the extent to which these occur but even if we were to agree we might still construct different explanations concerning these events.* In trying

---

* Official statistics concerning violence and hooliganism at football

to decide *why* certain things happen we are invariably thrown back on our conceptions of *what* is happening and our notion of what is happening depends on where we stand in relation to the social phenomenon under discussion. What we have done so far is simply to stand inside the phenomenon. We have listened to what fans say, we have looked at events on the terraces in close-up and on the basis of this we have outlined the social order and shared meanings which exist. We may still not *like* what is happening and what football fans do. We may continue to view the aggro leaders and hardcases as sad reflections of the violent society in which we live. We may equally view the nutters as pathetic attention-seeking figures unable to achieve social approval in any other setting. And we might be right. The fact that order exists is no guarantee that football grounds are nice friendly places to take one's aunty to. To draw a rather horrendous analogy we could point out that the extermination of four million Jews and two million gypsies in the concentration camp gas chambers of Hitler's Germany was a highly ordered and structured business. Victims were not killed by frenzied and anarchic savages. They were slaughtered on a terrifying scale by ordinary members of a state machinery in a very rule-governed and structured manner. The people who did the butchering were not animals but men and women with a set of perceptions and shared meanings which allowed the whole business to be justified and made rational, by absorbing it within a shared theory of men and society. Rituals of

---

grounds have to be treated with extreme caution. They are likely very much to reflect the changing attitudes on the part of the police to certain patterns of behaviour and their determination to do something about them. Despite this, however, the statistics make interesting reading. At Leeds United's ground the concern with hooliganism has been strong enough for the police to install an expensive remote-control video-camera system for crowd surveillance. At the same ground the total number of arrests made during the 1974 season was 273 – an average of about 9 per game. In terms of the total attendances at Leeds this works out at 0·02 per cent. At Oxford during the same season there were 83 arrests – an average of under 4 per game or 0·06 per cent of the total attendance. Of these arrests only five were for offences involving violence – the vast majority being to do with breaches of the peace of offences under the Public Order Act. During the 1974 and 1975 seasons the total number of injuries at Oxford United's ground which were treated by members of the St John's Ambulance Brigade was 311 – an average of about 7 per game or 0·1 per cent of the average attendance. Of these injuries over half were attributable to simple accidents such as falling down stairs or trapping fingers in gates. Out of those involving deliberate violence it was impossible to find any cases of 'innocent bystanders' being hurt and most of the injuries consisted of small cuts and bruises on the heads and faces of other involved Rowdies.

depersonalization practised on the incoming victims forced them to share in some aspects of the very theory in terms of which their extermination could be seen as justified.

The existence of order, then, does not, in itself, guarantee Utopia. The only way of deciding the merit or value to society of a particular order is through reference to the function of that order. We know that social order and a social rule framework existing within a subculture or microsociety bring about the creation and main-tenance of a set of social relationships (or is it the other way round?). But by function we refer to the 'work' that this social order does within a given culture or within cultures in general. Orders can consolidate a hierarchical network of social relationships which enable acts of almost unimaginable violence to be perpetrated. But they can also have functions which are very different.

It may appear that in our earlier concern with taking the notion of multiple realities seriously we have talked ourselves out of the possibility of ever putting forward truly functional explanations at all – appearing content to point out the orderly structure inhering in members' accounts and to present this structure as constituting one explanatory device. At this point, however, we wish to move from an examination of social realities to the formulation of an account of the genesis of the inside order. We do not pretend that the shift from structural (in a loose sense) explanations to functional theories is an easy one to manage, but some of the apparent conceptual problems may be removed by consideration of what we take to be some of the elements of an adequate social science.

Thus far the analysis has been in terms of inside and outside models. It has been suggested briefly that some aspects of the interactionist approach in the sociology of deviance may be able to account, at least in part, for the genesis of the outside model. The notion of social conspiracy has also been touched on in the expla-nation of the plurality of the Inside model. The origins of football matches, as opposed to other possible arenas, might possibly be explained in terms such as the increasing alienation of fans from what they perceive to be part of their traditional working-class heritage. As Ian Taylor has suggested, events at football matches can be seen as stemming from the increased professionalism in soccer and from the bid to turn the game away from its working-class connections towards a more sophisticated entertainment industry. We would reiterate, however, that theories of this sort need not be very powerful in their explanation of the social-historical origins of a particular 'problem'. The deviancy amplifi-cation model would seem to require only a small number of inci-dents (which might even arise by chance) in order to develop the familiar pattern of escalation.

At none of these levels, of course, are causal explanations of social action really legitimate. In appealing to the notions of careers or conspiracy one is not suggesting that there is any simple causal connection between such processes and what people do. We use the notion of rules, for example, as an explanatory device – a 'gloss' which is imposed on revealed structures in order to make sense of social behaviour. At the same time, we have suggested that rules, when made explicit by fans, can constitute reasons for their actions. Such reasons are offered in the context of justificatory accounts – e.g. 'I did that because it was expected of me'. The rule is offered as a legitimation of conduct, but there is an overpowering case for rejecting the naive idea that aspects of social behaviour are caused by or are unthinking responses to rules. (See Harré and Secord, *The Explanation of Social Behaviour*, p. 159.) It may be possible, however, that questions concerning causes might be legitimately posed at a very different level of analysis – that is, at the level of biology and physiology. In posing the question 'Why do we have orderly aggro of the terraces?' we might legitimately examine the possibility of this particular social order being founded upon some sort of 'natural' order. Equally, we could ask if members of various groups within society develop rule-governed solutions to aggressive conflicts because it is in their nature to do so.

There is a sense in which to pose the problem of relating a viewpoint – that is an explanatory account – to an underlying natural order is a logical absurdity. In examining realities the myth of the objective reality is largely abandoned. But, at the same time, room is left for one further reality – the reality which is constructed by the social scientist himself. This reality is in essence that which stems from the commonsense accounts of inside members but which is overlaid by an interpretative gloss imposed from the outside. Social action is explained in the football fans' own terms (as it must be), but in making a synthesis of justificatory accounts which members offer we inevitably transcend the terms of everyday language. The adequacy of this synthetic reality, which we see as constituting the primary stage of explanation, can be judged in two ways; first, on the basis of its fit with the commonsense reality of the inside social world and second in terms of the criteria which are used in the imposition of the interpretative gloss.

The account of the social world of the football fan which has been proposed rests on what fans themselves have to say. Stripped of its interpretative gloss, therefore, it must be intelligible and acceptable to fans. If one was to listen carefully to fans and on the basis of this build up an account of the inside reality but then found that this reality was unrecognizable when offered back to fans, one would have to admit that one had got it wrong. As Stan Lyman suggests, the best test of the accuracy of realities which sociologists and social psychologists portray is the ability of people to see themselves in the descriptions of their social worlds. In looking at the soccer culture we have taken his point seriously. In the research procedures attention has been given not only to the ways in which fans comment upon each other's accounts but also on the summaries and structures which we have pulled out of such accounts. In a number of cases it was pointed out that we had not got it right – that we had misinterpreted a particular gesture or had failed fully to grasp the subtle meaning of special language terms. The picture of the inside model was modified to accord with such corrections.

The ephemeral character of the classroom situation, which we explored vicariously in the work discussed in Chapter 2, prevented the completion of this process, just as it prevented us from making our own 'outside' view of what happened. All we could do was offer our interpretative gloss to another, similarly situated, group of fifteen-year-olds to see if they recognized themselves in action.

A point should be made here concerning participant observation. Many people seem to equate this kind of methodology with going along to events and simply looking at what goes on – they seem to leave out the participation bit. But an involvement, albeit a rather restrained one, in the action is a basic requirement. One needs not only to observe what is happening but also to *feel* what it is like to be in a particular social situation. This experiental aspect does not come about by being a totally disinterested onlooker. It comes about through an attempt to share in the excitement and emotions which, for soccer fans, constitute the 'electric' atmosphere which is seen as being the most important aspect of Saturday afternoons. There is nothing particularly 'scientific' about such experiences – they do not constitute data or allow for quantification. But on the basis of experience one is more able adequately to make sense of what fans have to say and the ways in which they describe their social world. There is a possibility of relating accounts to something which is personal rather than 'out there'. Now this does not mean that you can't do research into, say, vandalism without actually going out and kicking in a few windows – not at all. It is simply to point out that one is able to gain more insight into the world of a football fan by standing, with people one knows, in the Stretford End at Manchester or the London Road End at Oxford than by sitting in the comfortable seats of the covered stand or by looking through the viewer of a video-camera. There is little one can do as a social scientists purely on the basis of such experience. But at least there is a possibility that the more academic and rigorous explanations we offer have a meeting point with the lives of real people. We can never *know* what it is like to be a football Rowdy but we need not remain totally clueless.

On the basis, then, of constant checking and feedback from fans, coupled with an involvement in the soccer culture, we feel that the account of the inside model is reasonably accurate. The adequacy of the interpretative gloss, in contrast, is measured in a different way. The gloss consists, chiefly, of the imposition of concepts such as rules, careers and conspiracies, of which the notion of rules is the most fundamental. The adequacy of rules as an explanatory device, however, can be tested in quite hard and scientific terms. Bearing in mind the criteria we established earlier, one simply cannot take any 'problem' phenomenon, apply the rule-rhetoric and happily go home. If events are not rule-governed then the application of such a rhetoric will fail. If fans failed consistently to tell us, for example, that there are certain things one should not do in fights and conflict situations, then we would not want to argue a case for there being rules for fighting. Put simply, a rule structure cannot be manufactured out of thin air. It is either there to be revealed or it is not. In the same vein, since our notion of order rests on the demonstrable presence of rules, a sense of order cannot be imposed on activities which are disorderly.

In summary, the explanatory account we offer is not simply at the level of a personal view – a rhetoric which has the lowly status of an opinion or belief. It is firmly based on the commonsense meanings which fans share but it goes beyond this to place the meanings within a conceptual framework. Thus the plurality of accounts are seen within the context of social conspiracies. Roles are considered within the conceptual framework of careers. Most importantly, the justificatory accounts offered by fans are made sense of through the isolation of interpretative and prescriptive rules. However adequate such an explanatory model can be shown to be, though, a very different kind of objection to it can be raised. One might say that it is all very well to claim that events on the football terraces and in the school classroom are rule-governed and orderly but people still get stabbed and knocked unconscious, and property, both personal and public, is damaged and destroyed. There may be a tacit rule which proscribes the infliction of serious injury but we know that such injuries occur. Of what value is an analysis of rules when the things which concern most people in society are breaches of such rules? Such questions are rightly posed because one is dealing not only with a purely academic and scientific problem but also with a moral one. As academics, we can say that rules exist but from time to time they will be broken. If they were never broken they would be most unlike the rules with which we are usually acquainted. When people are seriously hurt it can often be shown that there has either been a breach of the rules or the rule-framework itself has been rendered less powerful by external events. As human beings, however, we are inevitably concerned with the implications and the effects of the explanations we offer. It is for this reason that we turn to a discussion of the possible function that 'aggro' plays in society, because it is through such considerations that the merit or otherwise of events at football matches and elsewhere might be gauged. It is through the concept of *ritual* that such functions might eventually be clarified.

Ritual

To propose that events on the football terraces constitute a contemporary example of ritual is to do little more, initially, than accord with the definitions of ritual offered by social anthropologists. Although definitions vary considerably from writer to writer it is possible to isolate a number of formal elements:
1   patterned routines of behaviour;
2   a system of *signs* which convey other than overt messages;
3   the existence of *sanctions* expressing strongly moral approval or disapproval;
4   a *conventional* relation between the actions in which the ritual is performed and the social act achieved by its successful completion.

These elements constitute what is usually described as ritual in a *broad* sense (see Firth, 1972). In a *narrow* sense, ritual would also be seen as involving magico-religious *rites* and symbolic action relating to the sacred. We will leave aside these aspects and concentrate on the broader conception of ritual, although it could be claimed that for soccer fans, football does indeed have a genuinely sacred aspect to it.

The broad definition constitutes what could be called a 'hard' concept since there are a number of strict criteria involved. To describe a social phenomenon as being a ritual is thus to apply a further interpretative gloss and to move to a higher level of explanation – in particular, to reveal the relation of the ritual to social acts in general and of the acts to other views of social reality. Now clearly we do not wish to say that because social action is orderly and rule-governed it is necessarily a ritual. But if we can show that in addition to rule-governed patterns of conduct there is also a distinct and identifiable system of symbols which communicate particular meanings within a microsociety, and in so doing accomplish certain social acts, then the explanations we can offer will be significantly enlarged. Having satisfied two of the criteria in the discussion of rules and social order it is to the aspects of symbolic communication that we now turn.

Football terraces are colourful places. They are rich in the emblems of allegiance, in scarves, banners, flags and even the slightly outmoded rosettes. All these objects communicate, at a glance, a very simple message – commitment to a particular football team. But there are more subtle messages which are communicated by gestures, by the manner in which one holds one's scarf and by the way in which one dresses. It is this latter medium on which we will concentrate here because in many ways it is the least obvious channel of communication. Most people seem to assume that one football hooligan looks much like another and that the clothes they wear convey little other than their identification with other trouble-makers. But things are by no means so simple. Although fans dress in a manner which accords with certain conventions and styles, they are still able to convey a wide range of messages in their choice of articles of clothing which fall within the wider conventions. In other words, the 'gear' which fans wear has a highly symbolic function. We have some empirical data to indicate precisely the kinds of messages which are communicated. These data arose out of a specific study which was involved, initially, with the isolation of the most frequent items of dress worn by fans and which went on to examine systematically the extent to which various combinations of dress items influenced fans' perceptions of the character and likely behaviour of the wearer.

The most frequently worn pieces of clothing, having been isolated from video-recordings and photographic stills, were taken as a set of sub-elements. From these a total of twenty-one water-colour paintings were made of a single fan dressed in various combinations of the clothing items. In one picture he would be wearing, say, a denim jacket, white baggy trousers and Dr Marten boots, whilst in another he might have had a combination of casual jacket, jeans and training shoes. Some pictures showed him with a scarf in a variety of positions – e.g. tied round the neck, knotted around the wrist, etc. – and in two cases he had a banner draped over his shoulders. In all cases the pictures looked realistic, both to us and the fans themselves.

The idea behind all this was that if the items of clothing, or combinations of items, had some symbolic function then fans should ascribe different characteristics to the fan depicted in the illustrations as a function of what he was wearing. The method used in pursuing this hypothesis was a variation on the repertory grid technique. Repertory grids, first developed by Kelly (1955), have a very important role to play in a social science which is directed towards an understanding of actors' conceptual systems because it involves very little in the way of imposed restraints or demand characteristics. It enables one to look at the way people generate concepts and apply them to the ordering of a range of elements – in our case, the set of pictures. The concepts can either be elicited during the procedure or they can be supplied by the investigator. The former allows for grids to be drawn up which are highly relevant to the person himself but which are difficult to handle statistically. When pseudo-constructs are supplied to the person the reverse is the case and personal relevance is sacrificed in order to achieve statistical convenience. In our study a combination of both approaches was used. First, a number of our informants were asked to describe, in their own terms, other fans on the terraces. The terms used in such descriptions were noted. Second, the pictures were shown to them and they were asked to describe the kind of people portrayed in more detail. From this material a total of twenty-one central constructs were isolated. They included items which related to the expected actions of depicted fans, e.g. 'Would stand and fight if things got rough on the terraces', and also a number of other attributes which emerged in fans' descriptions. These included such items as 'Regularly goes to away matches', 'Thinks he's hard but isn't', and 'Would get into a lot of trouble at school'. These constructs were then supplied to a further group of fans who were asked to rate each of the pictures on these criteria. They were also asked to supply any general comments they thought relevant and to indicate whether they thought that they would be 'friends' with the depicted fans.

The method may sound a little tortuous but it allows one to tease out, through statistical analysis a number of factors which summarize the way in which the constructs are applied to elements and the perceived 'distance' between each element. The factors which emerged were very interesting.*

First, fans attributed very different patterns of constructs to each of the 'target' elements. The fan depicted as wearing, say, white baggy trousers and boots was seen as being, in many salient respects, different from a fan wearing a denim jacket, jeans and shoes. There were many different expectations of the manner in which he would behave on the terraces, the extent of his loyalties to the club, or even his attitude towards school. Some of the pictures differed only in terms of a single article of dress (e.g. scarf tied around wrist rather than the neck) but even this small change was sufficient to change markedly the perception of the depicted fan's attributes and character.

---

* Analysis of the data was facilitated by a set of computer programs provided by the MRC service for grid analysis and produced by Dr Patrick Slater.

We can summarize the major results of this study as follows. The factors or dimensions which emerged were, first, a *'hardness'* dimension. Constructs relating to fighting and acts of courage were grouped together and summarized by this major component. Second, a dimension which related to *loyalty* appeared as being very important. And finally there was a factor which could be called a *'bullshit'* dimension. Labelling of such dimensions, which emerge from a factor analysis of the data, is of course, very difficult. But this job was made a little easier by the fact that fans had been asked to give general descriptions of each of the depicted fans. Thus by looking at how these elements were rated high and low on each of the major components it was possible to define the factors in fans' own terms rather than our own. We should point out that not all fans used the constructs in the same way but, very interestingly, the differences in their perceptions of the elements reflected very closely their own status and position within the microsociety. Novices had much less well-ordered conceptual systems in this respect.

The way in which the elements were discriminated from each other with respect to the components was strongly indicative of the powerful symbolic value of combinations of dress items and of certain items in isolation. Fans dressed in denim jackets, for example, were seen as being harder than the rest. Those wearing scarves were not surprisingly seen as being more loyal to the club. But those who wore them around the wrist were seen as being even more loyal and also very hard. Fans in combinations such as T-shirt, white baggies, scarf and flag were seen as being 'right hooligans' who, perhaps unexpectedly, came rather low down on the hardness scale. Of special interest were the fans depicted with no scarf at all. Those with a combination such as denim jacket, jeans and boots were seen as hard but not loyal. In contrast, other fans without a scarf but wearing casual jacket, trousers and shoes were consistently seen as being both hard and loyal. When we raised this rather anomalous finding with fans a rather interesting explanation emerged. Fans in the denim gear and boots are immediately identified as Rowdies. But Rowdies without scarves are seen as being both a little odd and not very loyal to Oxford United even though they might still be quite tough. The fans with the casual clothes were most often identified as Town Boys. As we know, Town Boys have already proved their worth both in terms of their hardness and their loyalty. The fact that they are not wearing a scarf is neither here nor there.

In general, it was clear that dress conveyed a great deal of information to fans even though they would have been unable to articulate very precisely what the messages were unless subjected to this somewhat gruelling procedure. There is some interaction between the items of dress and the persons wearing them, and the messages communicated will also vary in relation to the social knowledge and status of the receiver. But, on the basis of this evidence, coupled with the clear existence of a wide range of other more obvious signs, the criteria for establishing a ritual seems to be well met. Not only is action on the terraces orderly, it is overlaid with a rich system of signs conveying subtle but highly pertinent meanings.

Although the term 'ritual' is being used in a hard sense here it is reassuring to know that the term also accords with the everyday language of football supporters and many of the more informed sports writers have used the term quite freely (see, for example, 'The Tribe That Hides From Man' *(Foul Book of Football,* 1976)). At Oxford United, confirmation of the appropriateness of the term came in a rather amusing way. Towards the end of the fieldwork research period a reporter from the BBC came to the ground, walked up to a fan and, thrusting a microphone at him, said:

> 'There's a psychologist here who seems to think that the behaviour of football fans is really a big ritual – what do you have to say about that?'

The fan, who was not one who had been involved at all in the research programme, looked thoughtfully down at his Dr Marten boots for a moment, shuffled, raised his head, said, 'Yeah, that's right,' and strolled off. The kind of ritual we see occurring every Saturday during the football season has a number of clear analogues in other areas of social life and history. In fact, one of the major reasons for applying the ritual gloss to the social activities of soccer fans is that it allows such comparisons to be made more forcibly. If we examine the accounts of the Skinhead cult, the Mods and Rockers phenomenon or the Teddy Boys era we find very similar types of social order. We also find similar patterns of moral outrage and sanction developing with respect to such groups. Looking further back in history we find that at the race courses in the 1920s rival gangs fought out structured battles in a style which has much in common with contemporary ritual on the football terraces. And this aggro has more than a passing resemblance to the way in which war itself was conducted before the end of the nineteenth century. Robin Fox makes a similar comparison with respect to fights on Tory Island and provides us with this example:

> one is reminded of mediaeval warfare and of that great reformer Joan of Arc, who quite spoilt the whole thing. If you remember Shaw's St. Joan at least, you recall that she explains to the French Generals why they're not winning the wars and expects them to

be grateful for this information, instead of which they hand her over to be burned, because she was going to spoil all the fun. She explains that they were not fighting their wars to win, but that they were fighting their enemies to knock them off their horses and take them for ransom; to which the French Generals replied that that was what wars were about. War was not about killing all those peasants – one could do that at any time – war was about Knights. The lances they used were ridiculous. As people who set up tournaments and try to use them know, it was terribly difficult to manoeuver a lance, to do anything but simply knock someone off his horse. It was terribly difficult to do any damage to some-body protected by a ton of armour around him, and of course when he fell off he could not move and so was easily cap-tured. The whole thing was almost absurdly designed to this end.

If one looks at the mechanics and social processes of warfare right up to the end of the nineteenth century similar things seem to have been going on. War was about honour, character and ceremony as well as about economic and territorial gain. Killing was a part of warfare, but we have been misled by the gory Hollywood portrayals of events such as the Charge of the Light Brigade into thinking that massacre was an everyday event. Warfare was just as ritualized as fights on the football terraces or between Irishmen on Tory Island.

Looking at anthropological evidence the same kind of parallels can be drawn. Accounts of battles between rival groups of New Guinea warriors, for example, show that not only are such battles extremely ceremonial affairs but also that the sequential structure of conflict episodes is very similar to that observed on Saturdays in Britain. There are elaborate preparatory stages, stylized social means for the issuing and acceptance of challenges and a mode of fighting which seems almost guaranteed to inflict the least possible amount of death and injury in such situations. Consider this one small example from the account of battles among the Dani given by Gardner and Heider (1974);

Though fired with respectable velocity, the arrows do not fly true, since none are feathered. This is surprising in the light of the emphasis in Dani culture on birds, feathers and flight. A possible explanation may be that the Dani realize that if their arrows were feathered, many more warriors would be hit. Perhaps they know that even so small a change in the rules of war would disturb the delicate balance they have achieved between chance and com-petence, between competing needs of life and death.

The Dani, it would appear, have a greater understanding of the need for arms limitation than twentieth-century politicians.

Anthropological literature and histories of warfare are full of examples such as these. To ignore the obvious parallels between order at football matches and the ceremonial styles of battles and war, which have appeared in virtually all human societies throughout history, would not only be negligent but also quite contrary to the aims of a social science which seeks to construct explanations at different, but related, levels. Not only do rituals such as the one with which we have been concerned have the clear effect of limiting death and destruction, there seems to be something of a 'universal' character to them. Ritual aggro is by no means a novel invention of Western societies – it is just that people prefer to believe that the age in which they live is more violent and more destructive than the one before. Aggro, we would suggest, has always been an integral part of human cultures (see P. Marsh, *Aggro*, 1978). The fact that something very similar is present in the majority of other species of animal lends weight to the idea that the orderliness of aggro derives from a natural process which ethologists refer to as the *ritualization* of aggression.

It must be pointed out here that the terms 'ritual' and 'ritualization' have very different uses and implications. In contrast to the anthropologists' use of ritual, ethologists such as Sir Julian Huxley define ritualization in very different terms. It was Huxley, in fact, who coined the term and defined it as being 'the adaptive formalisation or canalisation of emotionally motivated behaviour, under the telenomic pressure of natural selection'. Among the functions of such a process, he maintained, was the reduction of intra-specific damage. At its simplest, certain patterns of agonistic behaviour are modified and differentiated through the processes of evolution of a species, and certain *threat* signals are evolved such that intra-specific conflicts become ceremonial in character – or, as Lorenz describes them, 'tournaments'. Somewhere along the line the real danger of fights, which even today occur for the age-old reasons of dominance, territoriality and access to receptive females, is removed and trials of strength and character pose little threat to the survival of a species. Huxley (1966) gives some short examples of how patterns of threat have evolved as a substitute for killing:

> During its ritualisation, the psychological effect of threat is enhanced by various means – exaggeration of apparent size or strength; bristling of fur or feathers; and additional conspicuousness of fighting organs. . . . In some lizards, threat through size-exaggeration has become mere bluff – but it works, and actual fighting never occurs. . . . In deer, antlers have a dual

function. They are so constructed that fights are very rarely fatal or even damaging. . . .

Huxley also goes on to point out that another method of ensuring that 'tournaments' provide the greatest degree of injury-reduction is the introduction of appeasement signals into the ritualized displays. The 'head flagging' in gulls described by Niko Tinbergen (1953) would be one example of such a signal which conveys capitulation and submission and effectively terminates the conflict sequence.

We could go on for a long time about ritualization in animals, but the field is well documented and enough has been said to illustrate the point we wish to make. Quite simply, we suggest that aggro is one contemporary social means available to man for coping with aggression. In other words, the *function* of aggro is precisely that of its analogues described by animal ethologists. Whilst animals may rely on instinctive patterns of motor co-ordination to direct their ritual displays of threat and submission, man develops social systems which rely on culture for their transmission. But the end-product is the same – order.

A discussion of ritualization allows us to make quite a sharp distinction between aggression and violence. As Lionel Tiger points out, violence is an event whilst aggression is a process. Violence is a consequence, but by no means an inevitable consequence of aggression. As we have shown in our studies of the classroom, aggression is by no means the only source of violence in human affairs. The subversion of personal pride and the systematic humiliation through long-term personal devaluation creates the conditions for violent reprisals to be acted upon someone unfortunate enough to be vulnerably present and patently active in the demeaning process. On the other hand, aggression might have any number of different outcomes depending on the context in which it occurs. Tiger (1971) sees the process as being conscious manipulation of the environment – a coercive force leading to change. And this view seems very reasonable when we consider the way in which the term aggression is used in everyday talk. We speak of the aggressive businessman trying to increase profits and win customers from his competitors. We also speak of the aggressive athlete who runs to win and to triumph over his rivals. And in our society we usually consider such men to be worthy of some praise and esteem. At the other end of the scale, aggression is the process which can lead, via special social and cultural conditions, to the wholesale killing and murder of other human beings.* It is the social conditions which

---

* It may very well be the case, however, that in the case of acts of extreme

mediate between aggression and its outcomes with which we need to be concerned – not with whether man is by nature a killer or a gentle pacifist.

Implicit in what we have been saying is the notion that aggression is inevitable. But this is not necessarily to commit ourselves to the idea that aggression, in any simple sense, is innate – only to the assumption that at one stage in our evolution it might have been so. We accept that, in all probability, there is something in the biochemical and neurological make-up of people which provides for an aggressive process but the actual arousal of aggression would seem to be very much a cultural affair. It seems no accident either that aggression in group contexts is strictly an all-male preserve – or at least it has traditionally been so. It might very well be that what Lionel Tiger calls 'male-bonding' originated early in the history of our species when men found it expedient to enter into co-operative bonds with each other in order to hunt more effectively. The only problem in accepting this view is that if this were the case then we would expect to see a continued association between male-bonding and killing. Instead, we see an association between the presence of all-male groups and ritual aggro. This current association is not predictable from an evolutionary process working to ensure the availability of food resources through hunting and killing. On the other hand, we might be wrong in assuming that the process of aggression, which in social terms finds its expression in the subduing of a rival, and that which stemmed from our hunting ancestry are discontinuous. Rather we might suppose that it is because the subduing of rivals has become ritualized that there is now a discontinuity in *outcomes* of the two processes.

Leaving this thorny problem aside, the phenomenon of aggression in all-male groups can be accounted for without recourse to genetic theories or to Hobbesian notions of man's inherent brutality. And it is here that the concept of positive feedback systems can be employed to some effect. Marvin Harris uses just this model in his account of the genesis and the persistence of male dominance, and his approach provides equally for an understanding of the fact

---

violence, such as massacre and genocide, certain remnants of a hunting background may become more involved and visible. We hold no brief for the 'Man the Instinctive Killer' philosophy of Ardrey and Lorenz, but it is quite reasonable to assume that certain social and cultural conditions may lead to the creation of certain categories of persons as 'Huntable'. Where this occurs features such as dehumanization will be present, and this in turn will lead to violence of a very destructive kind being seen as justifiable by those who regard the objects of their attacks as less than human. A further discussion of dehumanization occurs later in this chapter and in P. Marsh (forthcoming).

that it is men rather than women who are most centrally involved in aggro in our society.

We may suppose that at one time in our evolution men, for a variety of reasons, became predominantly responsible for the resolution of inter-group conflicts. It might have been because they were physically bigger and stronger or because their physiological constitution was such that they were more prone to make fierce attacks. But whatever the original reason it need not have been a very powerful one. For once males begin to take on this burden, women have little choice but to rear large numbers of fierce males in order to ensure a tribe's survival. (We note the large-scale killing of female babies which many societies, including our own, have practised.) The presence of fierce males, in turn, leads to an increased amount of warfare and this subsequently requires even more fierce males to be raised. Harris (1975) also notes a by-product of the feedback model:

> the fiercer the males, the more sexually aggressive they become, the more exploited are the females, and the higher the incidence of polygyny – control over several wives by one man. Polygyny in turn intensifies the shortage of women, raises the level of frustration among junior males and increases the motivation for going to war.

Now, it could well be that this is not an entirely correct interpretation of the processes which had led to male dominance and supremacy. We could probably arrive at the current position via a different route, and we could easily draw the feedback loop differently but still arrive at the same conclusion. The more important point to make is that the explanation of man's aggressiveness *today* need have little in common with the explanation of his becoming aggressive at an earlier point in evolution. This is true for the same reason that explanations of activities on the football terraces now need not be isomorphic with explanations of why the 'problem' came to soccer grounds in the first place.

To suggest that social order on the football terraces derives from a natural order is to hint at a functional explanation – a type of explanation we have been reluctant to propose at any other level. But, as we have shown, reference to a natural order does not mean that we wish to introduce the naive idea of inherited predispositions to act in a given manner. It might well be the case that certain genetic factors do influence what we do to some extent but such forces are probably very global and do not go beyond the undifferentiated constraints of hunger, sex and, possibly, aggression. If we ask why we have ritual aggro in society, we can point to its function of containing aggression. Fights are orderly because this enables them to have a symbolic and social force, thus ensuring the survival of a species. The fact that human beings have a strong urge to engage in sexual behaviour also ensures the survival of a species. But to suggest that men and women make love to each other for this reason would be as absurd as suggesting that boys and young men go to football matches with the expressed intent of retaining cere- monial solutions to inevitable and potentially injurious aggression. Social events, and social action which is given a particular meaning by actors, must be explained in social terms and in terms of reasons. But that need not prevent us from looking further afield, beyond the immediate circumstances of social situations, for an explanation of why a particular type of social event occurs in a variety of different cultures.

In undertaking a venture such as the one with which we have just been concerned it so happens that other features of football-terrace social life begin to take on a new relevance – a relevance which was not at all apparent at the level of an analysis of social rules and role positions. The discussion of aggression and its ritualization has touched on the concept of masculinity. Clearly, football games are attended by men and boys who watch other males kicking a ball around. But rituals on the terraces highlight the concern with mas- culinity in a very special way – that is, through the highly specific and structured manner in which insults are exchanged.

Ritual Insults

In the context of the football-terrace ritual a major objective of stylized insults is the denial of an opponent's masculinity. Consider the most frequent terms used for insulting a rival fan or even a player from the opposing team. Apart from what we might call 'dirty' words, e.g. shit, piss-face, etc., insults invariably include terms such as 'wanker', 'bugger', 'cunt', 'poofter', 'queer' and so on. These also happen to be the very terms used in school for someone who accepts the official definition of schooling (learning) and of social order within the classroom. The list, of course, is much longer than this, but a few examples will be enough to make the point.

The first term, 'wanker', is often accompanied by a flick- of-the-wrist gesture (especially when directed towards a group) which mimics the male masturbatory movement. It is probably the most frequent of all insult terms used at football games. To be called a wanker by someone is a very serious matter – it requires a response if made face-to-face, irrespective of who uses the term. It is

not something you can call a friend, even jokingly, whereas it would
be possible to call him a bugger. Bugger, although explicitly referring to an 'unnatural' sexual practice, is seen as being less insulting
than, say, 'queer' or 'poofter'. To call someone a queer is to imply
that he is not manly enough to be heterosexual, whilst a bugger
might still be O.K. with the girls. The term 'cunt' is the most
explicitly demasculinizing of all and is the most straightforward way
of inviting someone to fight. As we pointed out in the discussion of
terrace rules, simply to say 'cunt' as someone walks past is directly
to throw down the gauntlet to him. If he fails to respond and instead
of 'squaring up' like a man, runs away, the conception of him as
simply a female sex organ is reinforced. Such a situation might even
invite the further remark: 'He's worse than a cunt – a cunt's useful.'
These insult terms figure very prominently in chants and songs and
are an integral part of the ritual process. Again, there are literally
hundreds of examples of such chants to choose from – the following
are a tiny selection (see also Jacobson, 1975).

   '*Swindon Boys, Wank Wank Wank.*' This is one of the most clear
references to masturbation and is sung by Oxford United fans to a
fast but rather doleful tune. '*What a load of wankers*' and '*Oh he's a
wanker, he's a wanker*' are also chants which can be directed at rival
fans who might have engaged in a rather pathetic attempt to invade
one's End. They can also be directed against members of the opposing team, especially when they are losing.

   The term 'cunt' figures less in chants and songs, being reserved
mainly for face-to-face confrontations. Terms implying homosexuality, however, are very common indeed. At virtually every football game there is a specific ceremony for portraying the opposition's goalkeeper in this way. It takes place as he positions himself in
the goal in front of the fans' End, which may be either at the
beginning of the first or second half. The most common chant is
'*Danny – Danny La Rue*', but certain songs have the same aim in
mind. The following, for example, is often sung to a now outdated
pop tune and refers to the goalkeeper by name:

   Jennings dear, Jennings dear,
   Is it true what they all say
   That you are queer?

Goalkeepers, in fact, come in for a good deal of vilification generally because for half of the match they remain very close and
within earshot of the piece of terracing occupied by the Rowdies. At
times they are visibly affected by the stream of abuse which is
directed at them.

   Such stylized forms of insult clearly have the function of trying to
portray the opposition as effeminate. Conversely, some songs
encourage the image of one's own group as being manly and strong.

For example:
   'Oxford boys, we are here,
   Shag your women and drink your beer.'
The patterns of self-description and insult of rivals are not unique to the football terraces. Indeed, terms such as the few described (or their equivalent) crop up in virtually all examples of male single-sex groups, e.g. such rugby beer-drinking songs as 'The Good Ship Venus', etc. It is also interesting that there seem to be no equivalents among females in our society.

The ritual on the terraces, then, seems clearly related to the age-old problem of proving that one is better at being a man than one's rival. Fans on the terraces, unlike other animals, are not in direct competition for access to receptive females. So few women go to football matches that their efforts in this direction would go unheeded. But the need to demonstrate both dominance and masculinity is clearly present and it is through aggro that they can be achieved. It may be that the search for 'machismo' is a cultural left-over from the period in our evolution when selective breeding was something that was of some importance. Today, such selection is redundant and the Mr Universe figures are more likely to be found in magazines for homosexuals than those for women. Although football fans have a few ways of expressing their own potential heterosexuality, they are far fewer than the rituals for denigrating the masculinity of others. Being manly, for fans, is not simply to do with a reputation for sexual prowess, but rather is achieved through the contrast with rivals who are simply 'wankers' and unable to stand up for themselves in conflict situations.

The pattern of demasculinization, without a corresponding enhancement of one's own male sexuality seems to be an extremely important indicator of the type of violence which will ensue when groups who use such patterns come into conflict with each other. It would seem that some kind of portrayal of a rival as less than manly is a prerequisite for engaging in aggro towards him. In other words, there are two distinct stages to the ritual. The first consists of a repeated pattern of insults and denigration which portray rivals as feminine. Once this has been achieved, such rivals can be challenged, chased or even 'beaten up'. But the second phase usually stops short of serious injury. Compare this with what happens in other situations where violence of a very serious and damaging kind occurs. Whilst ritualized aggression is preceded by demasculinization, killing is preceded by *dehumanization*, for example during the Second World War Germans were portrayed as dogs or swine. Similarly, the North Vietnamese were given a variety of animal names or referred to in terms such as 'gook'. They were not people but rather something sub-human (see Kelman, 1973).

The fact that the process of dehumanization is largely absent in the conflicts between rival football fans provides a basis for cautious optimism. It suggests that the ritualization of aggression is effective and that the rules for fighting and for achieving dominance are intact. But there is a sense in which the rituals we have described are in some jeopardy. The fan who, in talking about the wrecked railway carriage, commented that the trouble started because the police were treating them like animals – so they behaved like animals – revealed the fragile nature of the football ritual. Rule frameworks and symbolic systems are not panaceas. They offer solutions to the problem of aggression only to the extent that others in society admit and recognize their value. Eventually, when the fines run into thousands of pounds and longer jail sentences are imposed on football rowdies, the pressure will be sufficient effectively to eradicate the whole phenomenon of the football hooligan. We are right to be concerned with acts of vandalism and assault, but if the official strategies for dealing with law breaking also take away the opportunities for boys and young men to engage in structured aggro, then we might very well be faced with a set of problems that are far more serious and much more difficult to control.

In this book we have not sought to excuse the football fan or the classroom trouble-maker. Instead we have simply tried to show that the events which outrage us have a different reality and are capable of being construed in a very different manner. We have tried to reveal social order in events which are traditionally seen as dangerously anarchic. And social order, whether it be in the form of ritual or not, is something that needs to be recognized and seen as having utility and merit. When magistrates and police refer to fans as animals and savages and when teachers are unwittingly engaged in the processes of systematic humiliation and depersonalization of schoolkids, order is threatened. We may never, given our existing social frames of reference, be able to create a system of schooling which kids regard as relevant to their own culture and socialization. And without doubt, we will be unable to suppress entirely the aggression and the striving to subdue rivals that has been characteristic of young males in all human societies at all times in history. Given this, we must look to ways of managing hostility and violence rather than naively hoping that they will go away. If we accept that there are, from one significant standpoint at least, *rules* of disorder, we might be able to develop management strategies which have far more purpose and effect than those which have currently emerged from the atmosphere of moral outrage and collective hysteria.

Bibliography

Becker, H. S. (1963), *The Outsiders* (New York, Free Press).

Bernstein, B. (1971), *Class, Codes and Control* (Routledge & Kegan Paul).

Cohen, S. (1972), *Folk Devils and Moral Panics* (London, MacGibbon & Kee).

Collett, P. (ed.) (1977), *Social Rules and Social Behaviour* (Oxford, Blackwell).

Corrigan, P. (forthcoming), *Doing Nothing* (London).

Creber, J. W. P. (1972), *Lost for Words* (Harmondsworth, Penguin).

De Saussure, F. (1974), *A Course of General Linguistics*, trans. Wade Baskin (London, Collins).

De Waele, J. P. and Harré, R. (1976), 'The personality of individuals' in R. Harré (ed.) *Personality* (Oxford, Blackwell).

Firth, R. (1972), 'Verbal and bodily rituals of greeting and parting' in J. S. La Fontaine (ed.), *The Interpretation of Ritual* (London, Tavistock).

Foul Book of Football (1976) (Foul publications).

Fox, R. (1977), 'The inherent rules of fighting' in P. Collett (ed.), *Social Rules and Social Behaviour* (Oxford, Blackwell).

Gardner, R. and Heider, K. G. (1974), *Gardens of War* (Harmondsworth, Penguin).

Goffman, E. (1961), *Asylums* (Harmondsworth, Penguin).

Goffman, E. (1963), *Stigma* (Harmondsworth, Penguin).

Goffman, E. (1971), *Relations in Public* (London, Allen Lane).

Harris, M. (1975), *Cows, Pigs, Wars and Witches* (London, Hutchinson).

Harré, R. and Secord, P. (1972), *The Explanation of Social Behaviour* (Oxford, Blackwell).

Huxley, Sir J. S. (ed.) (1966), 'Ritualisation of Behaviour in Animals and Man', *Philosophical Proceedings of The Royal Society,* Series B.

Jacobson, S. (1975), 'Chelsea rule – okay', *New Society* vol. 31, no. 651, March.

Kelly, G. (1955). *The Psychology of Personal Constructs* (New York, Norton).

Kelman, H. C. (1973), 'Violence without moral restraint', *Journal of Social issues,* vol. 29, no. 4.

Lang Report (1969), *Report of the Working Party on Crowd behaviour at Football Matches* (HMSO).

Lyman, S. and Scott, M. B. (1970), *A Sociology of the Absurd* (New York, Appleton-Century-Crofts).

Marsh, P. (1977), 'Dole queue rock', *New Society,* 20 January.

Marsh, P. (1978), *Aggro* (London, Dent).

Mead, G. H. (1934), *Mind, Self and Society* (University of Chicago Press).

Parker, H. (1974), *View from the Boys* (Newton Abbot, David & Charles).

Parsons, T. (1962), 'The school class as a social system' in A. H. Halsey, J. Floud and A. C. Anderson (eds), *Education, Economy and Society* (New York, Free Press).

Pollner, M. (1974), 'Sociological and common-sense models of the labelling process', in R. Turner (ed.), *Ethnomethodology* (Harmondsworth, Penguin).

Tajfel, H. (1972), 'Experiments in a vacuum', in J. Israel and H. Tajfel (eds), *The Context of Social Psychology: A Critical Assessment* (London and New York, Academic Press).

Taylor, I. (1970), 'Football Mad', in E. Dunning (ed.), *The Sociology of Sport* (London, Cass).

Taylor, I. (1971), 'Soccer consciousness and soccer hooliganism', in S. Cohen (ed.), *Images of Deviance* (Harmondsworth, Penguin).

Taylor, L. (1976), 'Strategies for coping with a deviant sentence' in R. Harré (ed.), *Life Sentences* (London and New York, Wiley).

Tiger, L. (1971), *Men in Groups* (London, Panther).

Tinbergen, N. (1953), *Social Behaviour in Animals* (London, Methuen).

Wilkins, L. (1964), *Social Deviance* (London, Tavistock).

Young, J. (1971), 'The role of the police as amplifiers of deviancy', in S. Cohen (ed.), *Images of Deviance* (Harmondsworth, Penguin).

Index